Speak English Around Town

Conduct Everyday Conversations with Confidence!

BOOK AND CD SET

AMY GILLETT

LANGUAGE SUCCESS PRESS

ANN ARBOR, MICHIGAN

Third Edition

Printed in the United States of America

ISBN: 978-0-9817754-7-0

Library of Congress Control Number: 2012906747

Illustrations by Evgeny Kran

Visit our website: www.languagesuccesspress.com

Bulk discounts are available. For information, please contact:

Language Success Press
2232 S. Main Street #345
Ann Arbor, MI 48103
USA

Email: sales@languagesuccesspress.com

Fax: (303) 484-2004 (USA)

Table of Contents

About the Author

Amy Gillett has taught English as a Second Language (ESL) and Business English in the USA and in Europe. Amy is also the author of the bestselling Speak English Like an American series, which includes *Speak English Like an American, More Speak English Like an American, Speak Business English Like an American, Speak Better Business English and Make More Money,* and *American College Slang*. Her writing has appeared in *Mad* magazine, *Family Circle*, and the *San Francisco Chronicle*, among other publications.

Amy majored in Slavic Languages and Literature at Stanford University and holds an MBA from Cornell University. She has studied and worked in many countries, including Russia, the Czech Republic, and Italy. Having studied eight languages, she is sympathetic to the struggles of the language student.

Acknowledgements

I would like to thank Jacqueline Gillett, ESL teacher *extraordinaire*, for all of her helpful advice and invaluable guidance in writing this book.

I would also like to thank my friends Tereza Typoltová and Lukáš Vítek from Prague. During their travels in the USA, they had many conversations with Americans that introduced them to new situations and expressions. Some of these interactions inspired material in this book.

Introduction

Welcome to *Speak English Around Town*. This book and CD will help you speak better English in your daily life — whether you're traveling around the United States, working with American colleagues, or socializing with Americans.

Speak English Around Town presents 325 American English idioms and expressions. You'll find these terms very useful for daily life.

All idioms in this book are shown in **bold**. Definitions of the idioms are included in each lesson and are listed in the Index. You'll notice that some words in the dialogues are in *italics*. These are words you may not understand. Check the Glossary on page 169 for definitions.

Each lesson has a "Language Lens" section, exploring a grammar point or structure. These points have been selected because they are tricky for non-native speakers.

Quizzes in each lesson let you test your new knowledge of both the idioms and of the Language Lens content. You'll find the answers in the Answer Key, starting on page 170.

You have a CD in your hands with all the dialogues. The CD will help you master the flow and rhythm of American English — how it's really spoken. The CD will also help you remember the idioms. Listen in your car. Play it on your commute. Download it to your iPhone or other mobile device and listen anywhere.

You're on the path to more fluent American English. And the great thing is, neither you nor I have any idea as to where this might lead. But we know that with your new language skills, new doors will open for you. Good luck speaking English around town, and enjoy your journey!

That style does run small.

GOING SHOPPING

Amy is at a clothing store shopping for a new pair of pants. Lisa, a saleswoman, asks her if she needs any help.

Lisa: May I help you?

Amy: I'm **just browsing**.

Lisa: Let me know if I can help. My name is Lisa.*

Amy: Do these pants **come in** black?

Lisa: Yes, but we're **sold out**. They're so popular, we can't keep them **in stock**.

Amy: Do you have any black pants **on sale**?

Lisa: Yes, these are **marked down** from $69.95 to $24.95.

Amy: That's a **good buy**, but **I'm not crazy about** the fabric.

Lisa: What about these pants? These are **on sale** for $49.

Amy: That's a little **pricey**, but I'll **try them on**.

(Amy enters the fitting room with the pants. A few minutes later, Lisa comes to check on her).

Lisa: How are the pants?

Amy: A little *snug*.**

Lisa: That style does **run small**. Let me bring you the next size up.

(Lisa hands Amy the pants and Amy puts them on).

Amy: These pants are a little big, <u>aren't they?</u>***

Lisa: No, they fit nicely!

Amy: They're *baggy* in the back, <u>don't you think?</u>

Lisa: No, they're perfect. **Take my word for it.**

Amy: I'm just not sure. I think I'd better **hold off** for now.

* Sales clerks often introduce themselves by giving their first name. They usually work on commission, so they get a percentage of the sale. When you check out, the cashier may ask, "Was anybody helping you today?" You tell the cashier the name of the sales clerk and he or she gets credit for the sale.

** Words in italics are defined in the Glossary on page 169.

*** Underlined material is the focus of the "Language Lens" section.

IDIOMS & EXPRESSIONS

(to) come in – to be available in; to be sold in a certain color, style, size, or material

• Does this jacket **come in** leather?

(a) good buy – a good price; a bargain

• You bought that Tommy Hilfiger shirt for just $15? That's a **good buy**!

(to) hold off – to wait to do something; to delay

• We'd like to buy a new car, but we're going to **hold off** until the new models are released.

in stock – available for sale

• If you're interested in that toaster, you should buy it now. We've only got a few left **in stock**.

just browsing – shopping, without necessarily buying anything; only looking

• "May I help you find something?" — "No, thanks. I'm **just browsing**."

---

marked down – lowered in price; on sale

• This shirt was **marked down** from $49.95 to $24.95.

(to) not be crazy about – to not like very much; to not be enthusiastic about

• I'm **not crazy about** your plan to spend all day at the mall.

---

on sale – at a reduced price

• I like this leather jacket, but $299 is expensive. I'll wait until it goes **on sale**.

---

pricey – expensive

• Lucia's Trattoria is a great restaurant, but it's **pricey**. Dinner for two costs about $150.

(to) run small / to run big – to fit small / to fit large (a cut or style of clothing that is smaller or bigger than expected)

• These shoes **run small**, so if you're usually a size 7, try an 8.

---

sold out – completely sold

• Gary went to the Apple store to buy the new iPad, but it was **sold out**.

---

take my word for it – trust me; believe me

• **Take my word for it**. You won't find this camera cheaper at any other store.

(to) try something on – to put something on to see if it fits

• You'd better **try on** your wedding dress again before the wedding to make sure it still fits!

✍ Practice the Expressions

Fill in the blanks with the missing word:

1) You look great in black. Take my word _____ it!

   a) in   b) for   c) with

2) This jacket is a good deal. It's marked _____ from $249 to $99.

   a) down   b) up   c) over

3) When the salesman asked if he could help me, I said I was just _____.

   a) searching   b) shopping   c) browsing

4) Sorry, the book you're looking for is not _____ stock. It's very popular.

   a) at   b) for   c) in

5) This shirt costs just $14.95. That's a good _____.

   a) buy   b) sell   c) purchase

6) We don't have any more striped scarves. We're sold _____.

   a) out   b) off   c) up

7) Does this sweater come _____ any other colors?

   a) with   b) from   c) in

8) Would you like to try that suit _____?

   a) up   b) on   c) in

9) Those shoes _____ big. Try the next size down.

   a) walk   b) run   c) skip

10) I'm not sure I need another pair of jeans. I'm going to hold _____ for now.

   a) off   b) in   c) up

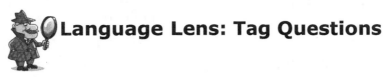# Language Lens: Tag Questions

Tag questions are short fragments at the end of a sentence. They turn a statement into a question. They are common in spoken English.

Note these uses and examples. The tag is underlined:
⇒ **To check if something is true**: You're going to the party tonight, <u>aren't you</u>?
⇒ **To ask for agreement**: We should bring a bottle of wine to the party, <u>shouldn't we</u>?
⇒ **To emphasize something**: Sara's certainly self-confident, <u>isn't she</u>?
⇒ **To make a request more friendly**: Open the door, <u>could you</u>?

If the verb in the main part of the sentence is positive (+), the verb in the tag is negative (-).

Main verb (+)	Tag verb (-)	Example
are ('re)	aren't	You're in good shape, <u>aren't</u> you?
should	shouldn't	We should go, <u>shouldn't</u> we?
can	can't	She can swim, <u>can't</u> she?
do	don't	You do love me, <u>don't</u> you?
'll be (will be)	won't	They'll be here later, <u>won't</u> they?

If the verb in the main part of the sentence is negative (-), the verb in the main part of the tag is positive (+).

Main verb (-)	Tag verb (+)	Example
're not (are not)	are	You're not coming, <u>are</u> you?
shouldn't	should	We shouldn't give up, <u>should</u> we?
can't (cannot)	can	We can't leave now, <u>can</u> we?
don't (do not)	do	We don't play with our food, <u>do</u> we?
won't	will	You won't cry when I go, <u>will</u> you?

Quick Quiz

Fill in the blanks with the correct tag:

Example:
You've got class tomorrow, _____?

Answer: You've got class tomorrow, <u>don't you</u>?

1) It's hot out today, _____?

2) Your father is a doctor, _____?

3) You're coming to my party, _____?

4) Your parents live in Florida, _____?

5) You were born in India, _____?

6) It's not raining out, _____?

7) You can't stay another day, _____?

8) You should call your mother, _____?

9) You can ski, _____?

10) We shouldn't bring our kids, _____?

RETURNING AN ITEM TO THE STORE

Paul bought a camera yesterday that doesn't work. He returns it to the store. Tim, the salesman, helps him make an exchange.

Paul: Hi, I bought this camera here yesterday, and it's not working.

Tim: Did you charge the battery and put it in correctly?

Paul: Yes. I followed the directions **to the letter**.

Tim: Do you mind if I **take a crack at** it?

Paul: **Be my guest**.

Tim: I usually **have the magic touch** ... Hmmm, you're right. It doesn't work. Would you like a *replacement*?

Paul: No, this is the second one I've had to return. I think I'll **steer clear of** this model.

Tim: **I hear what you're saying**. It's *frustrating* when you get one bad unit, **let alone** two!

Paul: Yeah, it's a **bummer**! I'd like my money back.

Tim: If you give me your receipt, I'll **issue a credit** to your credit card. But you might also try a different model or brand.

Paul: Maybe I will try a different camera.

Tim: We've got an excellent Canon camera that's the same price as this one. It would be an **even exchange**.

Paul: Okay, I'll take it. I hope this one **works out**.

Tim: If you're not happy with it, **don't hesitate to** bring it back.

IDIOMS & EXPRESSIONS

be my guest – please go ahead; try it yourself

• "May I try fixing the copier?" — "**Be my guest!**"

(a) bummer (slang) – a disappointment

• I lost my receipt, and the store won't take the dress back without it. What a **bummer!**

don't hesitate to – please go ahead and do something; don't be shy about doing something

• If you need advice on buying a car, **don't hesitate to** ask.

even exchange – a trade of equal value; when you return something and take something else that costs the same price

• If you return those pants and get this sweater instead, it will be an **even exchange**. They're both $39.99.

(to) have the magic touch – to have talent at doing something; to be able to do something difficult

• You can't open that bottle? Give it to Ivan. He usually **has the magic touch**.

I hear what you're saying – I understand you; I sympathize with you

• "I worked 60 hours this week. I'm exhausted!" — "**I hear what you're saying.**"

(to) issue a credit – to give money back to

• Rachel returned the sweater to the Gap, and the store **issued her a credit**.

NOTE: When a clerk issues a "store credit," the dollar amount is put on a store card that can later be used to buy something at that store.

let alone – much less; not to mention

• I can't remember the name of the movie, **let alone** the plot.

(to) steer clear of – to avoid, usually due to a bad experience

• Mark got food poisoning at O'Reilly's? We'd better **steer clear of** that place from now on!

(to) take a crack at – to try something

• I don't know if I can fix your laptop, but I'll **take a crack at** it.

---

to the letter – exactly

• I followed the recipe on the box **to the letter**, but this chocolate cake tastes terrible!

(to) work out – to be successful; to meet one's needs

• I just bought my first Mac. I hope it **works out**.

✍ Practice the Expressions

Fill in the blanks using the following expressions:

> take a crack at it   to the letter   has the magic touch
> let alone   what a bummer   steer clear of   works out
> issue you a credit   don't hesitate to   even exchange

1) This restaurant is lousy. Let's _____ it from now on.

2) You broke your leg in a skiing accident? _____!

3) Your toilet is broken. I'm not sure I can fix it, but I'll _____.

4) Installing this software is tricky, so be sure to follow the directions _____.

5) I barely have time to read a magazine article, _____ an entire book!

6) When it comes to making movies that kids love, Disney _____.

7) If you don't have your receipt, we can't give you your money back but we can _____.

8) I just bought a used car. I hope it _____.

9) If you'd like to return those pants and get these pants instead, it would be an _____.

10) If you have trouble setting up your new computer, _____ call me.

Language Lens: If Clauses to Talk About the Future

After the word "if," you usually use a **present tense verb** to talk about the future. The part of the sentence that contains the word "if" is the **dependent clause** and the other part of the sentence is the **independent clause**:

If you see something nice for Joan, please buy it.
    (dependent clause)   (independent clause)

Examples:
• If the weather <u>is</u> nice tomorrow, let's play tennis. (NOT: ~~If the weather will be nice tomorrow~~)
• If you <u>are</u> ever in Boston, give me a call. (NOT: ~~If you'll ever be in Boston~~)
• If we <u>have</u> time tomorrow, we'll go to the Metropolitan Museum. (NOT: ~~If we'll have time tomorrow~~)
• If I <u>win</u> the lottery, I'm going to quit my job. (NOT: ~~If I will win~~)

<u>Exceptions:</u>
⇒ **Use if + will** *(or the contraction 'll)* **for polite requests:**
• If you'll follow me, I'll show you to the restroom.
• If you'll be seated, we'll start the program.
• If you'll turn off your cell phones, the performance can begin.

⇒ **Use if + will** *(or 'll)* **to emphasize that you'll do something IF it will achieve a certain goal:**
• If it'll make you happy, I'll organize the party.
• If it will make Chloe stop crying, I will give her a piece of candy.

⇒ **Use if + will** *(or 'll)* **for indirect statements. Indirect statements start with clauses like "I don't know if" and "I'm not sure if":**
• I don't know if I'll be there.
• I'm not sure if I'll go tomorrow.
• Do you know if he'll be at the party?
• Who knows if I'll get an interview.

Quick Quiz

Fill in the blanks with the correct form:

1) If _____ in Chicago, I suggest you visit the Sears Tower.
   a) you're ever   b) you'll ever be

2) If Patrick _____ to Cornell, he'll definitely get accepted.
   a) applies   b) will apply

3) I don't know if my friend Marie _____ to the wedding.
   a) comes   b) will come

4) If the groundhog _____ his shadow next month, there will be six more weeks of winter.
   a) sees   b) will see

5) If _____ you happy, I'll get you that new video game for Christmas.
   a) it makes   b) it'll make

6) If _____ tomorrow, we'll have to postpone the picnic.
   a) it will be raining   b) it's raining

7) If _____ your cell phones, the concert can begin.
   a) you'll turn off   b) you turn off

8) If Joe _____ next Tuesday, who will show him around the city?
   a) will come   b) comes

9) I'm not sure if I _____ in the office tomorrow.
   a) am   b) will be

10) If _____ raining later, let's go play golf.
    a) it's not   b) it will not be

14

NEGOTIATING A PURCHASE

Max is shopping for a used car. He goes to see Jim, who's selling his used Honda. After a test drive, Max negotiates with Jim and gets him to reduce the price by $800.

Jim: Hello. Jim Harris speaking.

Max: Hello, Jim. My name is Max Taylor. I'm shopping for a used car, and I saw your ad for <u>a</u> 2008 Honda Civic.

Jim: <u>The</u> car is still available, but I'm getting lots of calls for it.

Max: How about if I **swing by** at 5:30?

Jim: Okay. I'm on 433 Main Avenue, across the street from Arroyo High School.

(Max comes over to Jim's house.)

Max: Hi, I'm Max. I'm here to see <u>the</u> car.

Jim: Good to meet you, Max. I'm Jim. Would you like to **take a test drive**?

Max: Yes, thanks. **The last thing I need is** another **lemon**!

Jim: You don't have to worry about that. This is <u>a</u> great car.

(They return from the drive.)

Max: It does drive well.

Jim: And it's **in mint condition**!

Max: You're asking $8,000 for it?

Jim: Yes, it's a **steal**.

Max: It's a nice car, but it's a two-door car and I was hoping to buy a four-door.

Jim: A car like this is going to sell quickly. I'd hate for you to **miss out**.

Max: I'll give you $7,000.

Jim: Let's **split the difference**. If you can make it $7,500, **you've got a deal**.

Max: I'd like to **sleep on it**. Can I **give you a ring** in the morning?

Jim: I'd like to **reach an agreement** now. How about $7,300?

Max: Would you take $7,200?

Jim: I don't want to **haggle**.

Max: I'm sorry to **nickel and dime** you, but **money is tight** for me right now.

Jim: Okay, let's **close the deal**. I'll take $7,200.

IDIOMS & EXPRESSIONS

(to) close the deal – to reach an agreement during a negotiation

• If you can take $5,000 off the price of the house, we can **close the deal** now.

(to) give someone a ring – to call someone on the telephone

• I'll **give you a ring** in the morning so we can make plans for tomorrow night.

(to) haggle – to argue over a price

• Greg **haggled** with the eBay seller and ended up saving $15 off the price of the guitar.

in mint condition – in excellent condition; like new

• David has a large collection of old comic books **in mint condition**.

lemon – a car that doesn't work well

• Molly's car is in the repair shop every month. What a **lemon**!

(to) miss out (on) – to lose an opportunity; to not experience

• Sara submitted her application too late and **missed out on** the opportunity to spend the semester in Paris.

money is tight – to not have a lot of money

• **Money is tight** for Paul and Wendy right now, with two kids in college.

(to) nickel and dime someone – two definitions:
1) to argue with someone over a small amount of money

• Mepstein Industries has a reputation for being cheap. People say they **nickel and dime** their suppliers.

2) to annoy someone by charging for every small thing

• Fred complained that the hotel **nickel and dimed** him by charging for local phone calls, Internet, and a pass for the gym.

(to) reach an agreement – to make an agreement

• We negotiated for several days before finally **reaching an agreement**.

(to) sleep on it – to take a day to think about a decision

• I can't give you an answer now regarding the job offer. I need to **sleep on it**.

(to) split the difference – to share a difference in cost 50-50

• You asked for a salary of $60,000, and we said the position paid $52,000. Let's **split the difference** and say $56,000.

(a) steal – a very good price

• You bought a new computer for $199? What a **steal**!

(to) swing by – to visit someone or a place for a short period of time; to make a quick visit

• I forgot my jacket at your house last night. Let me **swing by** after work and pick it up.

(to) take for a test drive – to drive a car to see how it runs

• Before he bought his new BMW, Jim **took it for a test drive**.

The last thing I need is – I definitely don't need; I really don't want

• I hope Rick and Jenny are planning to stay at a hotel when they visit town. **The last thing I need is** more houseguests!

you've got a deal – I agree; I agree to your terms

• You want $99 for that dining room table? **You've got a deal**!

✎ Practice the Expressions

Fill in the blanks using the following expressions:

swing by	in mint condition	you've got a deal
taking it for a test drive	miss out	split the difference
lemon	reach an agreement	steal	haggle

My car is a real _(1)_ and gives me a lot of problems. On Saturday morning, I looked online for used cars. I found a Mini Cooper listed. The ad said the car was purchased last year and was still _(2)_. Of course, I didn't want to _(3)_, so I called the number right away. The woman who picked up the phone introduced herself as Donna. She said, "I'm home right now. Can you _(4)_?"

I hurried over to her house. The car was a beautiful color and looked like new. Why was Donna selling it? "I don't want to sell it," she said, "but I'm moving to Japan in two weeks, and I can't bring it." After _(5)_, I knew I wanted it and I hoped we could _(6)_. I said, "You're asking $12,000 for this car and my budget is $10,000. How about we _(7)_ and say $11,000?" As you can see, I love to _(8)_.

"I'd like to close the deal, but that's too low," Donna replied. "This is a great car, and it's already a _(9)_ at $12,000." We negotiated for a few more minutes. When she offered to sell it to me for $11,600, I said, "_(10)_."

Language Lens: Articles

English has two types of articles: **definite (the)** and **indefinite (a, an)**.

⇒ Use **a/an** to refer to something **general** or **any member of a group**.

⇒ Use **the** to refer to something **specific** or a **particular member of a group**. When I say specific, I mean something that is known to both the speaker *and* the listener.

Compare these two examples from the dialogue:

1. I'm shopping for **a** used car. (Which used car? The speaker is not being specific).

2. **The** car is still available. (Both the speaker and the listener know which car. We're talking about a specific car now).

When to use the article "a" or "an":

1) Use "a/an" to refer to any member of a group.
Examples:
• I need a bike. (Any bike – it's not important which one).
• If you don't want to be alone, get a dog. (Any dog – it doesn't matter which one).

2) Use "a/an" to describe a person's job, what something is used for, or what type of thing something or somebody is.
Examples:
• Julia is a lawyer.
• This car is a two-door.
• She's a nice person.

3) Use "a/an" to speak about the general properties of somebody or something.
Examples:
• An infant requires a lot of attention.
• An unpaid parking ticket can lead to many problems.
• A beagle is a friendly dog.

4) Use "a/an" to describe a person in a general sense (if you don't know who the person is or if his or her individual identity is not important).
Examples:
• A woman came to the door while you were at the store. (Who? What woman? We don't know).
• I'm dating a lawyer.

When to use the article "the":

1) Use "the" when referring to something particular, specific, or unique.
Examples:
• The moon is bright tonight.
• The plane ride to France will take about 8 hours.
• The White House is a must-see if you visit Washington, D.C.

2) Use "the" when your listener knows which person, place, or thing you're referring to.
Examples:
• Please open the window. (Your listener knows which window — perhaps because you're pointing to it or because it's the only window in the room).
• The radio is still on. (Your listener knows which radio).
• What happened to the lawyer you were dating? (You're referring to a *specific* lawyer — someone you've already been told about).

When to use "the" and when to use no article:

1) Do not use "the" when talking about generalizations with plural or non-count nouns (for more on non-count nouns, see Lesson 17).
Examples:
• I like coffee in the mornings. (NOT: the coffee)
• Russian is a difficult language. (NOT: the Russian)
• Creativity is hard to teach. (NOT: the creativity)
• Pandas are popular animals. (NOT: the pandas)
Note: When the noun is singular and you're talking about generalizations, you will often use "the." Example: The panda is a much studied animal.

2) Most countries do not take "the": France, Australia, South Africa. Some countries do take "the" — especially those countries consisting of more than one word. *Examples:* the United States, the Netherlands, the United Arab Emirates, the Czech Republic, the Dominican Republic

3) States, cities, and towns do not take "the" except for "The Hague" and for a few towns in the United States. *Examples:* California, Paris, Westport, New Haven

4) The names of most lakes, mountains, volcanoes, and islands do not take "the." *Examples:* Lake Superior, Mount St. Helens, Mount Everest

5) Many expressions do not require "the." They include:
• at night (but: in the morning, in the afternoon)
• at/to college, school, work
• Transportation: by car, by foot, by plane, by train
• Days of the week and months of the year used with on or in: on Monday, on Tuesday, in December

DO use "the" in these cases:

1) For points of the globe. *Examples:* the South Pole, the Equator
2) For most geographical regions. *Examples:* the Midwest, the South, the Middle East
3) For names of oceans, seas, canals, and rivers. *Examples:* the Mississippi River, the Atlantic Ocean, the Black Sea
4) For forests, deserts, gulfs and peninsulas. *Examples:* the Gulf of Mexico, the Black Forest, the Arabian Peninsula

Quick Quiz

Fill in the blanks with the correct article (a, an, the) or choose "no article" if no article is needed.

1) You're going to Italy? I have _____ uncle who lives in Rome.

  a) an   b) the   c) no article

2) We're going to _____ Lake George for two weeks in August.

  a) the   b) a   c) no article

3) John wants to become _____ doctor.

  a) the   b) a   c) no article

4) We're going to _____ Czech Republic. What towns should we visit?

  a) a   b) no article   c) the

5) At _____ night, I like to read a book and drink _____ cup of herbal tea.

  a) no article ... a   b) a .... no article   c) no article ... the

6) _____ Nile is _____ longest river in _____ world.

  a) The ... the ... the   b) The ... the ... a   c) A ... no article ... the

7) Emily will definitely get into Yale. She's _____ excellent student.

  a) no article   b) an   c) the

8) I'm going shopping tomorrow. I need _____ new suit.

  a) no article   b) a   c) the

9) We're going to Chicago by _____ car.

  a) no article   b) a   c) the

10) I only drink _____ coffee in _____ morning.

  a) a ... the   b) the ... no article   c) no article ... the

I don't need any of those bells and whistles.

BUYING A SERVICE PLAN

Tom is shopping for a new cell phone plan. It's tricky because there are many options. Mike, a salesman at the cell phone store, helps him choose the right plan.

Tom: Hi, I'm **in the market for** a new cell phone plan.

Mike: Do you have a plan now?

Tom: Yes, with MobileOne. But it's about to *expire*.

Mike: You're not happy with them?

Tom: No, I'm not. Their service is terrible. My calls are always **breaking up**.

Mike: Cellular Star's service is **first rate**. You'll get great *reception*. What are you looking for in a plan?

Tom: I need 400 minutes a month for daytime calls. I'd like unlimited night and weekend calling.

Mike: What about call forwarding, voice mail, and text messaging?

Tom: I don't need any of those **bells and whistles**.

Mike: The Choice 450 is our **no-frills** plan. That'll **run you** $39.99 a month, plus tax.

Tom: That doesn't include long-distance calls, does it?

Mike: Yes, it does.

Tom: So it's $39.99 a month, plus tax.

25

Mike: Yes, and there's a **one-time fee** of $35. That's for **setting up** the account.

Tom: Any **hidden fees**?

Mike: No. Of course, you'll want to read **the fine print** of your contract.

Tom: Right. I don't want to **get stuck with** a plan that only lets me make long-distance calls between midnight and 3 a.m.

Mike: Did I mention that if you sign up for this plan by Friday, we'll **throw in** a free phone?

Tom: I **could use** a new phone.

Mike: It's a great offer, with **no strings attached. All set to** sign up?

Tom: Before I **sign on the dotted line**, I'd better make sure I know what I'm **getting into**.

IDIOMS & EXPRESSIONS

all set to – ready to (do something)

• The salesman at the Gap asked, "**All set to** check out?"

bells and whistles – product features which are attractive, but not essential for the product to function

• I just want a reliable car. I'm not looking for a lot of **bells and whistles**.

(to) break up – to lose a phone signal; to start losing a phone connection

• I can barely hear you. We're **breaking up**.

could use – need; have use for

• Your ties are all stained. You **could use** some new ones.

(the) fine print – the part of a contract with special rules and limitations. These are often "hidden" in small print, which is why you'll often hear: "Be sure to read the fine print."

• Julie didn't read **the fine print** of the fitness club contract carefully, and now she's stuck with a lifetime membership.

first rate – of the highest quality

• If you're looking for a restaurant, I recommend the Mediterranean Grill. The food there is **first rate**.

NOTE: You will also hear the term "second rate" to describe something that is of inferior quality or not very good.

(to) get into – to get involved with (often used in a negative sense, as when one has gotten involved with something that is now unpleasant or not wanted)

• My evening MBA program is more demanding than I thought it would be. What have I **gotten into**?

(to) get stuck with – to have something unwanted or undesirable that one cannot get rid of

• I'm in charge of cleaning the bathroom once a week at our dormitory. I don't know how I **got stuck with** this task!

hidden fees – extra charges that are not made clear from the beginning

• When you sign up for a new credit card, make sure there are no **hidden fees**.

in the market for – shopping for; interested in buying

• We're **in the market for** a flat-screen television.

no-frills – a simple and basic service or product

• If you want to fly cheaply, try a **no-frills** airline like Ryanair.

NOTE: "frills" are extra features or benefits

no strings attached – with no limits or special demands attached (to an offer)

• Kim got a full scholarship to Stanford, **no strings attached**.

---

one-time fee – a charge that you only pay one time

• To join FitOne Gym, I had to pay a **one-time fee** of $199, then a monthly membership fee of $49.

(to) run you – to cost you

• It's going to **run you** $600 for a one-year membership to Club Five Fitness.

(to) set up – to establish; to arrange; to put something new in place

• I **set up** direct deposit so that my paychecks are automatically deposited into my bank account.

(to) sign on the dotted line – to agree to or sign up for something (often by signing a contract or agreement)

• I'm interested in joining the gym but before I **sign on the dotted line**, can you please explain the cancellation policy?

(to) throw in – to include for no additional fee

• If you sign up for a one-year gym membership today, we'll **throw in** a free set of towels.

✎ Practice the Expressions

Fill in the blanks with the missing word:

1) A new Honda Civic will run _____ $16,000 with tax.

   a) you   b) at   c) on

2) Did you read the _____ print before signing the contract?

   a) small   b) little   c) fine

3) Can you recommend a simple DVD player — one without all the _____ and whistles?

a) buttons   b) bells   c) rings

4) When I ordered tea from the Aroma Tea Shop, the company threw _____ a free sample of some oolong tea.

a) up   b) in   c) on

5) Charlie was _____ set to order a cappuccino at Starbucks before he realized he forgot his wallet at home.

a) ready   b) every   c) all

6) A real estate company in Florida is making a special offer: buy a house and get a new car, no _____ attached.

a) roof   b) strings   c) threads

7) Be sure to read the contract carefully before signing on the _____ line.

a) solid   b) thick   c) dotted

8) If you're looking for a hotel in Manhattan, I recommend the Pierre. It's _____ rate.

a) first   b) second   c) fine

9) Club Five Fitness is no-_____. They don't even provide towels.

a) thrills   b) frills   c) fills

10) We thought our car rental would cost $100 a week, but it ended up costing $200. There were lots of _____ fees.

a) hiding   b) hidden   c) secret

Language Lens: Negative Questions

Negative questions can be used to:

⇒ **Confirm that something is true or has happened.** You are assuming something is true and you are just checking.
Example: You didn't tell Ted we think he's a lousy boss, did you? (Expected answer: No, I didn't).

⇒ **Express surprise that something hasn't happened**
Example: Haven't you mailed that letter yet? (Note that this can often express annoyance. The person asking the question is annoyed that the other person did not do something).

⇒ **Offer a polite invitation**
Examples:
Won't you come in?
Wouldn't you like some coffee?

Study these examples for ways to answer negative questions:

Didn't you see the car coming?
– Yes, I did. (Do <u>not</u> just say "yes" in response to this type of question. Give a complete answer: "Yes, **I did**.").
– No, I didn't. (You may also say just "no" without "I didn't.")

Aren't you hungry?
– Yes, I am. / Yes, I'm starving!
– No, I'm not. / No, I just had breakfast.

Won't you sit down?
– Yes, thank you.
– No, I've only got a minute.

You're not tired after your trip?
– Yes, I am tired. (Do <u>not</u> just say "yes.")
– No, I'm not tired. (Note here that you're saying "No…" even though you are agreeing with the person who asked the question. You're confirming that you're not tired.)

Quick Quiz

Part A: Practice answering negative questions:

Example: Didn't you get my e-mail? (You didn't)

Answer: No, I didn't.

1. Don't you like spinach? (You do)

2. Don't you want to rest before dinner? (You don't)

3. Didn't she understand the joke? (She didn't)

4. Aren't they on vacation in Italy? (They are)

5. Isn't he graduating this year? (He isn't)

Part B: Turn these statements into negative questions:

Example: I think we're going in the wrong direction.

Answer: Aren't we going in the wrong direction?

1. You're moving to San Francisco.

2. They're going to New York today.

3. You're thirsty.

4. You want another piece of pizza.

5. She broke her arm.

Why don't we flag the waiter down?

ORDERING AT A RESTAURANT

Tanya and John go to Carmen's Bistro for dinner. It's Saturday night and the place is packed! Finally, Kevin, their waiter, comes to take their order.

Tanya: I hope the waiter comes soon. **I'm starving!**

John: Me too!

Tanya: <u>Why don't we</u> **flag him down**?

John: Waiter, waiter!

Kevin: **I'll be right with you!** ... Sorry for the **hold up**. We're **packed to the rafters** tonight.

John: We noticed!

Kevin: I'm Kevin, and I'll be your *server* tonight. **Can I start you off with** some drinks?

John: I'd like the Sam Adams Summer Ale.

Tanya: **Make it two**.

Kevin: And did you **decide on** some appetizers?

John: We're going to **skip the appetizers** tonight. What do you recommend for a main course?

Kevin: We're **known for** our seafood. The salmon with black bean sauce is our most popular dish.

Tanya: Okay, I'll try that.

Kevin: Excellent choice. And for you, sir?

John: I'm having trouble deciding. I'm **in the mood for** steak, but I know you **pride yourselves on** your seafood.

Kevin: <u>How about trying</u> the **surf and turf**? That way, you get **the best of both worlds**!

John: Okay, **<u>let's</u> go with** that.

Kevin: I'll be right back with your drinks. They're **on the house** because you had to wait so long to order.

IDIOMS & EXPRESSIONS

(the) best of both worlds – the advantages of two things

• Waitressing in the evenings gives Sue **the best of both worlds**: she can attend classes during the day and still earn money.

Can I start you off with ___? – Would you like to start your meal with ___?

• Welcome to Amici's. **Can I start you off with** some drinks?

(to) decide on – to choose

• "Did you **decide on** a main course yet?" asked the waitress.

(to) flag down (the waiter/waitress) – to get the attention of the waiter/waitress

• You want another glass of wine? Let's **flag down** the waitress.

hold up – delay; long wait

• We ordered 20 minutes ago. What's causing the **hold up**?

NOTE: See Lesson 23 for the verb "to hold up."

I'll be right with you – I'm coming in a minute

• "**I'll be right with you**," said the waitress when she saw me waving to her.

I'm starving – I'm very hungry

• When we asked Jim why he ordered two steaks, he said, "**I'm starving**."

in the mood for – to want; to have an appetite for

• Let's go to a seafood restaurant. I'm **in the mood for** fish.

known for – famous for; having a reputation for

• Chicago is **known for** its delicious pizza.

let's go with – I'll take; let's proceed with

• You recommend the Chardonnay? Okay, **let's go with** that.

make it two – I'll have one too; I'll have the same thing (as the other person just ordered)

• "I'll take a cappuccino." — "**Make it two**."

on the house – free; paid for by the restaurant

• The waitress offered us after-dinner drinks **on the house**.

packed to the rafters – really crowded

• Beth's Bistro is always **packed to the rafters** on Saturday nights. If we want to go there, we'd better make reservations.

(to) pride oneself on – to be known for; to be especially proud of something

• San Francisco **prides itself on** its fine restaurants.

(to) skip the appetizer(s) – to not order appetizers

• We're not that hungry, so we're going to **skip the appetizers**.

surf and turf – a meal containing both meat and seafood

• The waiter said, "Tonight, our special is the **surf and turf**. It comes with a lobster tail and a New York strip steak."

🖎 Practice the Expressions

You are a waiter (or waitress) at Anita's Restaurant. Choose the appropriate replies to your customers (remember: be polite — you like your job and want to keep it!):

1) Customer: "You guys are packed to the rafters tonight."

Your reply:
a) "Yes, there's plenty of seating available."
b) "Yes, we can seat you up in the rafters if you want."
c) "Yes, I'm afraid there's going to be a 30 minute wait for a table."

2) Customer: "We've been waiting forever for you to come and take our order!"

Your reply:
a) "Sorry about that. Let me get you some drinks on the house."
b) "You still haven't decided? I'll come back in a few minutes."
c) "Sorry. I was busy helping everybody who came in after you."

3) Customer: "We're going to skip the appetizers tonight."

Your reply:
a) "The calamari is our best appetizer."
b) "Okay, have you decided on a main course?"
c) "Okay, should I just bring the dessert menus?"

4) Customer: "I hope your portions are big. I'm starving!"

Your reply:
a) "Then I suggest our house salad. It's very light."
b) "I recommend just getting an appetizer then."
c) "I suggest the lasagna. It's a very large serving."

5) Customer: "What do you suggest? I'm in the mood for fish."

Your reply:
a) "Try the filet mignon. It's our best steak."
b) "The stuffed chicken special is excellent."
c) "Try the blackened tuna. It's delicious."

6) Customer: "I hear you pride yourselves on your steak."

Your reply:
a) "Yes, we're very proud of our steak."
b) "Yes, we do have steak on the menu."
c) "Yes, our customers are proud to order our steak."

7) Customer: "I can't decide between the fish and the steak."

Your reply:
a) "Then I suggest you spend more time thinking about it."
b) "Then I suggest you try our vegetarian special."
c) "Then I suggest the surf and turf."

8) Customer: "I've been trying to flag you down for the past 10 minutes. Didn't you see me waving?"

Your reply:
a) "Yes, I saw you but I thought you were just saying hello."
b) "No, I'm sorry I didn't notice. It's very crowded here tonight."
c) "No, but I saw you raising your hand."

9) Customer: "Why did you bring us both glasses of red wine? My wife asked for white wine."

Your reply:
a) "I thought she said, 'make it two' when you asked for a glass of white wine."
b) "I thought she said, 'make it two' when you asked for a glass of red wine."
c) "I thought you said, 'a glass of red wine for me and a glass of white wine for her.'"

10) Customer: "We've been waiting 45 minutes for our meals. What's the hold up?"

Your reply:
a) "Sorry. Your meals will be right out."
b) "There's no hold up. Everything is fine."
c) "You got to the restaurant late."

Language Lens: Making Suggestions

These are three great ways to make suggestions:

1) Why don't we / you / I + base form of the verb*

Examples:
• Why don't we go out for pizza?
• Why don't I drive you to the airport on Friday?
• Why don't we got out to dinner on Saturday?
• Why don't you call the movie theater to see what time the show starts?

* Note: The base form of the verb is the verb without any endings. Examples of verbs in the base form are: run, eat, play, go, find

2) How about + -ing form of the verb

Examples:
• How about going sailing this weekend?
• How about inviting the Smiths over for a barbeque?
• How about studying some French before our trip to Paris?
• How about getting Chinese takeout* for dinner?

* Takeout is food you order in a restaurant and take with you, to eat at home, in your office, or somewhere else.

3) Let's + base form of the verb

Examples:
• Let's take a walk on the beach.
• Let's work on the project tomorrow.
• Let's wait and see how the weather is before making our plans.
• Let's get tickets to a Broadway play.

Quick Quiz

**Turn the following phrases into suggestions using:
why don't we / how about / let's:**

Example:
watch a Woody Allen movie
(why don't we)

Answer: Why don't we watch a Woody Allen movie?

1) eat lunch at the mall
(let's)

2) look for a birthday present for Marina
(why don't we)

3) get some burritos for dinner
(how about)

4) visit the Picasso exhibit at the Metropolitan Museum
(let's)

5) go to Martha's Vineyard in July
(why don't we)

6) get a subscription to *New York* magazine
(let's)

7) show me how to use Skype
(how about)

8) see a performance at Carnegie Hall
(why don't we)

9) order Korean food for dinner
(why don't we)

10) go to Italy this summer
(let's)

Loud music in restaurants is a pet peeve of mine.

COMPLAINING AT A RESTAURANT

At Carmen's Bistro, all is not going well. John complains to Kevin, the waiter, about his overdone steak. Tanya complains that her fish is too rare and that the music is too loud.

Kevin: How are we doing?*

John: Not very well. I ordered my steak **medium rare**, and it's **burnt to a crisp**!

Kevin: I'm sorry about that. I can ask our chef to prepare another one.

John: Okay, please do that.

Kevin: **You bet**. And how's your fish, ma'am?

Tanya: It's very rare.

Kevin: Would you like me to have the chef put it back in the oven?

Tanya: No, I've **lost my appetite for** fish.

Kevin: I'd be happy to bring you something else.

Tanya: Okay, let me try the stuffed chicken breast.

(Ten minutes after the waiter has brought the new meals.)

Kevin: How are we doing over here?

Tanya: <u>I was wondering if</u> you could **turn down the music**. Loud music in restaurants is a **pet peeve** of mine.

Kevin: Sure, I'll take care of that. Can I get you another **round of drinks**?

41

John: No, we're **all set** for now.

(The waiter returns after 15 minutes.)

Kevin: Are you still **working on** your meals?

Tanya: I'll need a **doggy bag**.

John: <u>Would you mind</u> **wrapping this up**, too?

Kevin: I'll bring you some containers, and you can **box up** your **leftovers**. **Can I interest you in dessert**?

Tanya: I'm **stuffed**.

John: <u>Could you</u> please bring the check?

* Sometimes waiters will ask, "How are we doing?" instead of "How are you doing?" This sounds very friendly and informal.

IDIOMS & EXPRESSIONS

all set – not needing anything else

• When the waitress asked if we needed anything else, we told her we were **all set**.

(to) box up – to put leftover food from a restaurant in a container

• It looks like you've got a half a hamburger left. Would you like to **box that up**?

NOTE: In the USA, the trend is for restaurants to give customers a white container ("box") and have them put their own leftovers in it.

burnt to a crisp – completely burnt; very overcooked

• Joe put the hamburgers on the grill and then forgot about them for an hour — no wonder they're **burnt to a crisp**!

Can I interest you in dessert? – Would you like to order dessert?

• When the waitress asked, "**Can I interest you in dessert?**" I replied, "Yes, we'll take a look at the dessert menu."

doggy bag – a bag or container to take home food that a customer could not finish at a restaurant

• This salad was huge. I'm going to need a **doggy bag**.

leftovers – food that is not eaten at a meal; extra food that is eaten later

• After our big Thanksgiving dinner, we had **leftovers** for three days. We were all sick of eating turkey by then!

(to) lose one's appetite – to not want to eat any more due to a bad experience

• After finding a hair in her soup, Andrea **lost her appetite**.

medium rare – cooked just past the raw stage

• This steak is overcooked. I ordered it **medium rare**, but it's brown in the middle.

pet peeve – an annoyance; a particular thing that bothers someone more than the average person

• Paul hates it when people talk on their cell phones while driving. That's his **pet peeve**.

round of drinks – drinks for a whole group

• Ed offered to buy all of his friends at the bar a **round of drinks**.

stuffed – to be completely full

• After eating five pieces of fried chicken each, we were all too **stuffed** to eat any dessert.

(to) turn down the music – to lower the volume of the music

• I can't hear you. Can you please **turn down the music**?

(to) work on – to eat; to finish eating

• When the waitress asked me if I was finished with my lobster, I said, "No, I'm still **working on** it."

(to) wrap up – to put in a container or box (to take home)

• Sue didn't finish her meal so she asked the waiter to **wrap it up**.

You bet – yes; no problem

• "If this DVD doesn't work in my DVD player, can I return it?" — "**You bet**."

🖎 Practice the Expressions

You did well on the exercise in Lesson 5, and you still have your job as a waiter/waitress at Anita's Restaurant. Choose the appropriate replies to your customers:

1) Customer: "The music is so loud, we can't hear each other speak."

Your reply:
a) "Let me turn up the music."
b) "Let me turn down the music."
c) "You'll need to speak louder."

2) Customer: "Can we get another round of drinks over here?"

Your reply:
a) "Sure. I'll bring the check right away."
b) "Sure. What would you like?"
c) "Sure, but first you should finish what's in your glasses."

3) Customer: "This fork is dirty. Dirty silverware is a pet peeve of mine."

Your reply:
a) "Right. I don't like pets in restaurants either."
b) "Sorry about that. Let me bring you a clean fork."
c) "I don't mind dirty silverware either."

4) Customer: "There's a hair in my soup. I just lost my appetite!"

Your reply:
a) "Sorry. Let me get you a fresh bowl of soup."
b) "Sorry. I forgot to mention we serve all our soups with hair."
c) "Sorry. Let me just reach in and remove it for you."

44

5) Customer: "I ordered my steak rare, but this is burnt to a crisp!"

Your reply:
a) "I'm sorry. Let me tell the chef to put it back in the oven."
b) "I'm sorry you don't like burnt meat."
c) "I'm sorry. Let me have the chef prepare another one for you."

6) Customer: "The pasta was good, but now I'm stuffed!"

Your reply:
a) "I'll let you relax for a while before bringing the dessert menu."
b) "Okay, then let me bring the dessert menu right away."
c) "I'm sorry you didn't get enough to eat."

7) Customer: "This steak was delicious, but I couldn't finish it."

Your reply:
a) "Should I throw it in the trash for you?"
b) "Should I put it on a new plate and serve it to somebody else?"
c) "Should I wrap it up for you?"

8) Customer: "I'll need a doggy bag."

Your reply:
a) "We don't allow dogs here."
b) "I'm not surprised. The portions are big here."
c) "I'm glad you were able to finish everything."

9) Customer: "I'm still working on my dessert."

Your reply:
a) "Okay, let me take your plate away."
b) "Okay, I'll be back in a few minutes to check on you."
c) "Okay, I'll bring the check right away."

10) Customer: "We're all set here."

Your reply:
a) "Okay, I'll bring more drinks."
b) "I'll let the chef know."
c) "Okay, I'll bring the check."

Language Lens: Polite Requests

Use one of these phrases to make polite requests:

- Could you (please)
- Would you mind
- I was wondering if you could

Here's how to form the sentences:

⇒ **Option A: Could you + base form* of verb + "?":**

Examples:
- Could you pick up a pizza on your way home from work?
- Could you help me translate this letter?
- Could you please** drop my book off at the library?

* The base form of the verb is the verb without any endings
** The "please" here is optional. Of course, it makes the request more polite.

⇒ **Option B: Would you mind + [verb + ing] + "?"**

Examples:
- Would you mind picking up a pizza on your way home from work?
- Would you mind helping me translate this letter?
- Would you mind dropping my book off at the library?

⇒ **Option C: I was wondering if you could + base form of verb + "."**

Examples:
- I was wondering if you could pick up a pizza on your way home from work.
- I was wondering if you could help me translate this letter.
- I was wondering if you could drop my book off at the library.

Note that Options B and C are less direct than Option A and therefore may sound a little more polite.

Quick Quiz

Turn the following phrases into requests, using the words in parentheses:

Example:
drive me to work tomorrow (would you mind)

Answer: Would you mind driving me to work tomorrow?

1) feed our dogs while we're away (I was wondering if + could)

2) pick me up from the airport on Friday (I was wondering if + could)

3) borrow your car (I was wondering if + could)

4) return my library book (I was wondering if + could)

5) loan me your laptop (would you mind)

6) turn down the music (would you mind)

7) pick up my clothes from the dry cleaners (would you mind)

8) show me how to design a website (could you)

9) please let Jim know we're running late (could you)

10) call the theater and reserve tickets (could you)

Come back here? When hell freezes over!

PICKING UP THE TAB AT A RESTAURANT

It's time to pay the bill at Carmen's Bistro. Tanya and John discuss who will pay it. Then they talk about how much to tip.

Tanya: Let me **pick up the tab**.

John: No, **it's my treat**. The guy is <u>supposed to</u> pay on a date!

Tanya: Says who? I don't want you to pay for me every time we go out! Let's **go Dutch** this time.

John: No, I'll get it. **I insist**.

Tanya: Okay, but next time **it's on me**.

John: Let's see ... The total without tax is $74.75.

Tanya: Do you think we should leave 15 percent* or more?

John: The service was **so-so**. Our waiter was **no great shakes**. He seemed **put out** when we complained about our food.

Tanya: What did he expect? The food **left a lot to be desired**! This is <u>supposed to be</u> such a great restaurant. I don't know what happened.

John: I guess it's **gone downhill**. I'll leave 15 percent. I could leave less, but I don't want to be a **cheapskate**!

Tanya: Yeah, we may want to come back here someday.

John: Come back here? **When hell freezes over!**

* It's standard to tip waiters and waitresses 15-20 percent in the U.S. They are unhappy when they get less than 15 percent.

IDIOMS & EXPRESSIONS

cheapskate – someone who doesn't like to spend money; a cheap person

• Dana is such a **cheapskate**. She brings her own tea bags to restaurants and asks for a cup of hot water.

(to) go downhill – to become worse over time; to deteriorate

• The service at the Seaside Bar & Grill has really **gone downhill**. We waited 45 minutes for our food to arrive!

(to) go Dutch – to split the bill

• Amanda didn't want her boyfriend to pay the entire restaurant bill, so she suggested they **go Dutch**.

I insist – I will pay (say this when you do not want to argue anymore over who will pay the bill — it's usually the last word)

• "Dinner is my treat." — "No, you paid last time. I'm paying tonight. **I insist**."

it's my treat – I'll pay the bill

• "Let me pay for dinner tonight." — "No, I invited you to dinner, so **it's my treat**."

it's on me – I'll pay

• Put your wallet away. **It's on me**.

(to) leave a lot to be desired – to be bad or lacking in some way

• Josh chews with his mouth open and rests his elbows on the table. His table manners **leave a lot to be desired**.

no great shakes – not so good; fair; unimpressive

• The person we just interviewed for the job was **no great shakes**. I think we can find somebody better.

(to) pick up the tab – to pay the bill

• Everybody left the bar before the bill came, so I was stuck **picking up the tab** for our entire group!

put out – annoyed; inconvenienced

• Joel seemed really **put out** when I asked him if he could drive me to the airport.

so-so – average; not very good

• Paul and Nora weren't thrilled with their tour of Portugal. It was just **so-so**.

When hell freezes over – never

• Will the boss invite us all over to his house for dinner? **When hell freezes over**.

🖎 Practice the Expressions

Fill in the blanks using the following expressions:

pick up the tab	**went downhill**	**let's go Dutch**
when hell freezes over	**it's my treat**	**cheapskate**
so-so **on me**	**leaves a lot to be desired**	**put out**

Kara: I had a date last night with Steve, that guy I met online last week. We went to that new restaurant downtown, Zanzibar.

Leah: How was the restaurant?

Kara: It was (1) . The appetizers were good, but my fish was lousy.

Leah: So what did you think of Steve?

Kara: Things were going okay, until the bill came. Then things (2) . When the bill came, he suddenly seemed (3) .

Leah: Why? He's not used to getting a bill at a restaurant?!

Kara: He looked at it and then said, " (4) ."

Leah: He made you pay for your own meal? What a (5) !

Kara: So I told him, "No, dinner is (6) ."

Leah: You're kidding? You offered to (7) ?

Kara: Yes, I offered and he accepted.

Leah: Wow! Such cheap behavior (8) .

Kara: At the end of the evening, he did say, "Next time we go out, (9) ."

Leah: And when will you be going out with him again?

Kara: (10) !

Language Lens: Supposed to

Use "supposed to be" when talking about something that is generally thought to be true.

Examples:
• Paris is **supposed to be** the most romantic city in the world.
• Your boyfriend took you to dinner at Masa? That's **supposed to be** the most expensive restaurant in the city!

Use supposed to + infinitive to:

⇒ Say what should or should not be done because of rules, common practices, or customs

Examples:
• Before ordering supplies, you're **supposed to** get your boss's approval.
• You're not **supposed to** smoke inside this restaurant.

⇒ Express sarcasm and/or anger, in place of should, can, or going to

Examples:
• Who was the nineteenth president of the United States? How am I **supposed to** know? (= I don't know! How would I know?)
• Your music is so loud, how am I **supposed to** get any work done? (= How can I get any work done with that loud music? I can't!)
• You invited your entire office over for dinner? Who's **supposed to** do all the cooking? (= I don't feel like cooking for all those people! Who's going to do all the cooking?)

⇒ Express something that was planned or intended, but did not happen (in this case, use "was/were supposed to")

Examples:
• Luke **was supposed to** start college in the fall, but then he decided to travel around the world instead.
• We're lost! We **were supposed** to take a right onto Danbury Road.
• We **were supposed** to go to a holiday concert last night, but it was snowing too hard.

Quick Quiz

Re-write the following with "supposed to":

Example: If you keep talking to me, how am I going to concentrate?

Answer: If you keep talking to me, how am I supposed to concentrate?

1) How can I do my homework when it's so noisy in the house?

2) Weren't you going to tell me when it was time to get off the highway?

3) Who's going to do all the cooking for the big party you're planning?

4) Who's going to clean up this mess?

5) We were planning to go to London last month, but the trip got canceled.

6) I've heard Venice is the most beautiful city in Europe.

7) If you want to take vacation time, you need to get permission from your boss.

8) Amanda and I were going to meet yesterday, but she canceled the meeting.

9) Who's going to clean all these dishes in the sink?

10) You can't take flash pictures inside the museum.

ORDERING LUNCH TO GO

Joe goes to Angelo's Sandwich Shop to get a sandwich. After speaking with Tim, the clerk, he decides on the meal deal.

Tim: Welcome to Angelo's. **What can I get for you?**

Joe: A chicken salad sandwich.

Tim: **For here or to go?**

Joe: To go.

Tim: <u>Would you like</u> that on white, wheat, or pumpernickel?

Joe: What's pumpernickel?

Tim: It's a dark brown bread, similar to rye bread.

Joe: Let me try that.

Tim: And <u>would you like</u> that with mustard, mayonnaise, or oil?

Joe: Mustard. But please **go light on** it.

Tim: <u>Would you like</u> to make that a **meal deal**? Our special this month is a sandwich, an order of French fries, and a large soda for $6.99.

Joe: I'm going to **pass on** that. But <u>I'd like</u> a **side order** of fries.

Tim: **Your total comes to** $6.99.

Joe: **On second thought**, I will **take you up on** that **meal deal**.

Tim: Sure, then you'll get a soda **at no extra charge**. That'll be $6.99.

Joe: Sorry, but I've only got a $100 bill.

Tim: **No worries**. We can **break** it.

IDIOMS & EXPRESSIONS

at no extra charge – free with a purchase; for no added fee

• Bob and Susan will only stay at hotels that let them bring along their dog **at no extra charge**.

(to) break – to make small change

• Can you **break** a $50 bill? I don't have anything smaller.

For here or to go? – Do you want to eat in the restaurant or take the food with you?

• "**For here or to go?**" — "For here, please."

(to) go light on – to put on just a small amount

• Please **go light on** the mayonnaise.

meal deal – a promotion in which several food items are sold together at a good price

• If you're hungry, I recommend the **meal deal**. You get a sandwich, soup, and drink for just $8.99.

no worries – don't worry about it; that's fine

• "There's a 45-minute wait to get a table." — "**No worries**. We'll just order our food to go."

on second thought – I changed my mind

• I'm not going to order dessert. **On second thought**, the chocolate lava cake sounds delicious. I'm going to order that.

(to) pass on – to say no to; to reject

• I'm going to **pass on** dessert. I'm stuffed.

side order – a smaller dish served with the main course

• I'd like a **side order** of onion rings with my hamburger.

(to) take you up on – to accept your offer

• You're inviting me to lunch today? I'll **take you up on** that.

> **What can I get for you?** – What would you like to order?
>
> • "**What can I get for you?**" — "I'd like the meal deal."

> **your total comes to** – the bill is; the amount you owe is
>
> • "**Your total comes to $12.89.**"

✍ Practice the Expressions

Fill in the blanks using the following expressions:

> your total comes to   at no extra charge   go light on it
> side order   what can I get for you   for here or to go
> pass on   on second thought   no worries   meal deal

Cashier: Welcome to Dan's Sandwich Shop. __(1)__?

Sandra: What does the __(2)__ come with?

Cashier: A sandwich, your choice of soup or salad, a drink, and a cookie.

Sandra: I'm going to __(3)__ that. It sounds like too much food. I'll take a turkey sandwich with a __(4)__ of French fries.

Cashier: Mustard or mayonnaise on the sandwich?

Sandra: Mustard, but __(5)__.

Cashier: Is this __(6)__?

Sandra: To go. __(7)__, I'll have a salad instead of the sandwich.

Cashier: __(8)__. I'll just go ahead and change that. I'm going to include a cookie __(9)__. __(10)__ $8.50.

# Language Lens: "Polite" Would

Use "would + like" to make polite requests or to ask a question in a polite way. The contracted form of *would* is *'d*. When speaking, you'll usually use the contracted forms (I'd, you'd, he'd, we'd) instead of the full forms (I would, you would, he would, we would).

Requests:
• I'd like another cup of coffee, please.
• I'd like another few days to finish the proposal.
• We'd like another bottle of wine.
• We'd like a room with a view.

Polite questions:
• Would you* like some more coffee?
(You could also say, "Do you want some more coffee?" but using "would" makes the question more polite).
• Would you like to stay for dinner?
(You could also say, "Do you want to stay for dinner?" but again, using "would" makes it more polite).
• Would you like some help with your luggage?

* Note that "would you" is often pronounced as one word: *wouldja*.

Ask "wouldn't you like" if you want a positive response:
• Wouldn't you like to stay for dinner? (This sounds more like you really do want someone to stay rather than just asking, "Would you like to stay for dinner?").
• Wouldn't you like another cookie? (You're encouraging the person to go ahead and take another one).

Quick Quiz

Turn the following into polite requests using "'d like" (the contracted form of "would like"):

Example: I want a ride to the movies tonight.

Answer: I'd like a ride to the movies tonight.

1) I want that report on my desk by 5 o'clock.
2) I want a cup of coffee.
3) I want to leave early on Friday.
4) I need another pillow.
5) Give me some help with this project.

Form questions based on these situations using "would you like":

Example: Your wife says she has no time to cook dinner tonight.

Answer: Would you like me to cook dinner tonight?

1) Your friend keeps looking at his empty coffee cup and then at the full pot of coffee on your counter.

2) Your neighbor tells you that her car is in the repair shop and she has no way to get to work tomorrow.

3) Your sister calls to tell you that her babysitter just canceled and she has nobody to look after her kids tonight.

4) It's 11 a.m. You're leaving the office. Your boss asks where you're going. You answer, "To get coffee at Starbucks." He replies, "I love their cappuccinos."

5) Your friend asks what you're doing to celebrate Thanksgiving. You say you're having a dinner at your house. You ask what she's doing, and she says, "I have no plans."

I'd like to help you, but my hands are tied.

MAKING A DOCTOR'S APPOINTMENT

Grace is sick. She calls her doctor's office to make an appointment for today.

Laura: Primary Medical Group. How may I help you?

Grace: I'd like to make an appointment with Dr. Feinberg.

Laura: Your name?

Grace: Grace Lee.

Laura: **What's the nature of your visit?**

Grace: I think I've **come down with** the flu.

Laura: We **have an opening** tomorrow at three.

Grace: I can't wait that long. I'm really sick!

Laura: Well, unfortunately, Dr. Feinberg is **booked solid** today. <u>If he were free</u> **at all**, <u>I would</u> **squeeze you in.**

Grace: Can anybody else see me?

Laura: **Hang on.** Let me check ... You're **in luck**. Dr. Wilson can see you at four o'clock this afternoon.

Grace: Don't you have anything earlier today?

Laura: No, **I'm afraid not**. We're **short-staffed** this week.

Grace: So there's no way I can come in before four today?

Laura: I'd like to help you, but **my hands are tied**. <u>If I were you, I would</u> grab this four o'clock appointment.

Grace: Okay. I'll take it.

61

IDIOMS & EXPRESSIONS

at all – to any extent; in any way

• "Did Kelly help organize the party?" — "No, she was no help **at all**."

NOTE: You will also hear "not at all," meaning "not in any way." "Example: "Is it a problem for you to come to the office on Saturday?" — "No, **not at all**."

---

booked solid – unavailable; having all appointments taken

• We wanted to stay in the Palace Hotel during our stay in Prague, but it was **booked solid**.

(to) come down with – to become ill with; to catch a sickness

• Your throat hurts and you feel warm? I hope you're not **coming down with** something!

---

hang on – wait; give me some time

• The phone is for me? **Hang on**. I'll be there in a minute.

(to) have an opening – to have an available space in a schedule

• Olivia is sick. I'm going to see if her doctor **has an opening** for this afternoon.

I'm afraid not – sorry, but I can't do that

• "Can you give me a ride to the airport on Saturday morning?" — "No, **I'm afraid not**. I have other plans."

---

in luck – lucky; fortunate

• You want to see the football game on Saturday? You're **in luck**! I've got an extra ticket.

---

my hands are tied – there's nothing I can do

• I'd like to give you more time to finish the test, but **my hands are tied**.

short-staffed – without enough staff; having less staff than usual

• Sorry you had to wait so long. We're **short-staffed** today.

(to) squeeze someone in – to make an appointment available

• You want an appointment for a haircut today? I can **squeeze you in** with Lynn at 3 o'clock.

What's the nature of your visit? – Why are you coming?; Why do you need to see the doctor?

• You want to see Dr. Patel? **What's the nature of your visit?**

✎ Practice the Expressions

Fill in the blanks with the missing word:

1) You want to come in for a massage this afternoon? We can squeeze you _____ at five o'clock.

   a) out   b) in   c) up

2) I'm sorry. We can't give you an appointment until tomorrow morning. We're short-_____ today.

   a) footed   b) staffed   c) handled

3) If you don't get a flu shot, you might come _____ with the flu.

   a) up   b) away   c) down

4) When I arrived at the doctor's office, the receptionist asked, "What's the _____ of your visit?"

   a) nature   b) matter   c) reason

5) Sorry, I'm going to have to give you a speeding ticket. I'd like to give you a break, but my _____ are tied.

   a) feet   b) fingers   c) hands

6) Jane: "Can you loan me $1,000 to pay my rent this month?"
Joe: "No, I'm ____ not."

a) afraid   b) scared   c) worried

7) Does Dr. Collins have any ____ tomorrow?

a) open   b) openings   c) closings

8) We wanted to have dinner at Aquavit during our stay in New York, but unfortunately the restaurant was ____ solid.

a) reserved   b) busy   c) booked

9) You want to see Dr. Garcia this afternoon? Hang ____. Let me see if she's available.

a) up   b) on   c) in

10) You're ____ luck. We had a cancellation so Dr. Garcia will be able to see you at 3 p.m. today.

a) in   b) on   c) with

Language Lens: Present Unreal Events

When we talk about events that are wished for, imagined, or unreal, we often use the if/would structure. Even though we are talking about the present, the verb in the *if clause* is put in the past tense. This form is called the conditional.

> **Form it like this:**
> If + verb in past tense, <u>would + base form of verb</u>
> *(or 'd)*

Examples:
• If you liked football, I would invite you to the game on Saturday.
The meaning here is that you do NOT like football, so I will not be inviting you to the game.

• If Ben studied harder, he'd get into Harvard.
In other words: Ben won't get into Harvard because he doesn't study hard enough.

• If we had a lot of money, we'd buy a vacation home in Vermont.
But we do not have a lot of money. Therefore, we won't be buying that vacation home!

When the verb "to be" is in the *if clause*, use "were" instead of "was." This is called the subjunctive mood. "If I were you" is often used to give advice (you are imaging yourself in somebody else's place or situation). The next time you want to give advice to someone, remember to say, "If I were you..." and NOT "If I was you."

Examples:
• If I were the boss, this office would be a lot more fun.
• If I were you, I'd buy a new suit for the interview.
• If I were you, I'd apply right away for that position.
• If I were you, I'd join Match.com and start dating again.

Quick Quiz

Fill in the blanks with the missing word or words:

1) If I _____ a cat, I would sit by the window all day.

   a) was   b) were   c) would be

2) If I were you, I _____ a hybrid car.

   a) would buy   b) am buying   c) bought

3) If I _____ younger, I'd take a job overseas.

   a) were   b) would be   c) am

4) If I were in charge, I _____ everybody leave early today.

   a) let   b) would let   c) am letting

5) If I were you, I _____ looking for a new job.

   a) start   b) started   c) would start

6) If I _____ someone to go with, I would go to the dance tonight.

   a) have   b) had   c) will have

7) If Pam _____ more friendly, she wouldn't have such a hard time making friends.

   a) were   b) was   c) will be

8) If Chris called his mother more often, she _____ happy.

   a) will be   b) were   c) would be

9) If you _____ harder, you'd get a promotion.

   a) will work   b) work   c) worked

10) If you _____ opera, I would take you to see Don Giovanni at the Metropolitan Opera.

   a) would like   b) like   c) liked

VISITING THE DOCTOR

Grace has an appointment with Dr. Wilson. After discussing her symptoms and giving her a check-up, he says she has the flu.

Doctor: Hi, I'm Dr. Wilson. **What seems to be the trouble?**

Grace: I've been **under the weather** for days.

Doctor: The flu is **going around**. Did you get the vaccine?

Grace: No, this year I didn't **get around to it**.

Doctor: What are your symptoms?

Grace: I've had a **splitting headache** since yesterday morning. My whole body hurts.

Doctor: You have all the **telltale signs** of the flu. Let me take your temperature … 101. That's **on the high side**.

Grace: My throat hurts, too.

Doctor: Let me **take a peek**. Yes, your throat is very red. It looks like a **garden-variety** flu.

Grace: Are you going to prescribe some medicine for it?

Doctor: You can take Tylenol for your headache. Also, be sure to get plenty of rest and drink lots of water.

Grace: How long do you think this is going to **drag on**?

Doctor: You should be **back on your feet** in a week **or so**.

Grace: I have to get better quickly! I'm needed at the office.

Doctor: Well, there's **no magic bullet**. You're going to have to let this **run its course**.

IDIOMS & EXPRESSIONS

back on one's feet – healthy again; returned to good health

• I was sick for two weeks, but now I'm **back on my feet**.

(to) drag on – to last too long; to last longer than one wants

• I've had a cold for three weeks. It just keeps **dragging on**!

garden-variety – ordinary; common; not unusual

• The necklace that Jim bought his girlfriend is not a **garden-variety** piece of jewelry. It cost $100,000.

(to) get around to it – to have a chance to do something; to have time to do something

• I know I need to have my cholesterol checked, but I just haven't **gotten around to it**.

going around – spreading; going from one person to another

• Your stomach hurts? You must have caught the bug that's **going around**.

magic bullet – a drug or therapy that cures or prevents an illness, without harmful side effects; a simple solution to a problem (usually one that is too simplistic and doesn't work)

• Bedbugs are very hard to get rid of. Unfortunately, there's no **magic bullet**.

NOTE: this is often used in the negative: "no magic bullet"

on the high side – rather high

• Emma stayed home from school yesterday because her temperature was **on the high side**.

or so – approximately (referring to a time period or quantity of something)

• There were 200 **or so** people at the conference.

(to) run its course – to allow time for an illness to pass through one's body

• There's no cure for the cold. Just let it **run its course**.

splitting headache – a very bad headache

• Julia left work early, saying she had a **splitting headache**.

(to) take a peek – to have a quick look

• Your car isn't running well? Let me **take a peek** under the hood and see if I can figure out what's wrong.

telltale signs – sure signs of a problem; typical symptoms that indicate something

• Liz feels nauseous all the time and says she's gaining weight. Those are **telltale signs** that she's pregnant!

under the weather – feeling sick

• If you're **under the weather**, don't go to work.

What seems to be the trouble? – What's wrong?

• "**What seems to be the trouble?**" asked the auto mechanic when we brought our car in to the shop.

✍ Practice the Expressions

Imagine that you are at the doctor's office. Choose the most appropriate replies to the doctor:

1) Are you feeling under the weather again today?
   a) Yes, I woke up with a headache.
   b) Yes, I'm feeling much better than yesterday.
   c) Yes, I see several storm clouds in the sky.

2) Get plenty of rest and let this cold run its course.
   a) Right. I'm planning on going running this afternoon.
   b) Okay, I'm glad to hear the cold will go away so quickly.
   c) Okay, I'll stay home from work for the next couple of days.

3) A runny nose and a sore throat are telltale signs of a cold.
   a) I thought I might have a cold.
   b) I knew I didn't have a cold.
   c) I thought it might be cold out today.

4) Unfortunately, there's no magic bullet for Lyme Disease.
   a) Okay, please write me a prescription for it.
   b) Right, I understand it can be difficult to treat.
   c) Right, bullets don't cure anything.

5) What seems to be the trouble?
   a) It's no trouble at all.
   b) My left ear has been hurting for several days.
   c) Things are going very well.

6) Your temperature is 100 degrees. That's on the high side.
   a) That's good news.
   b) I thought I was feeling a little warm.
   c) I thought I was feeling a little cool.

7) A stomach bug is going around.
   a) I think I must have caught it.
   b) I don't know where it's going.
   c) I'm glad it's going around.

8) What do you usually take when you have a splitting headache?
   a) I take aspirin or Tylenol.
   b) I take a couple days off work.
   c) I don't take anything because it doesn't hurt.

9) You've got a garden-variety cold.
   a) Oh no! How will I ever recover?
   b) Okay. I'm glad it's nothing serious!
   c) How could I have caught such an illness?

10) Your cough shouldn't drag on too much longer.
   a) So you think it'll last another couple of months?
   b) So you think I'll have it forever?
   c) So you think it'll be gone by next week?

Language Lens: Going to / Will

In spoken English, "going to" is the form used most often to talk about the future.

⇒ **Use "going to" to talk about something planned for the future:**
• I'm going to buy a new car this year.
• Is your daughter going to attend Dartmouth or Columbia?
• What are you going to do on New Year's Eve?

⇒ **Use "going to" to make a prediction based on evidence you have now:**
• Be careful. You're going to spill your drink!
• This plan is too complicated. It's not going to work.

"Will" is also often used to speak about the future. Use will *(or 'll)* **in these situations:**

⇒ **To talk about a decision made at the moment of speaking.**
Once you've made the decision, use "going to" to talk about it:
• I'll make the dinner reservations for Saturday night. Bob, please let Sara know that I'm going to make the dinner reservations.
• Mom: "Zach, if you don't go to bed right now, I'm not taking you to the zoo tomorrow morning!"
  Zach: "I'll go to bed now! Dad, I'm going to go to bed now."

⇒ **To talk about things we believe to be true about the future:**
• I'm sure you'll like your new job.
• The dean will serve for five years.
• Our new toaster will arrive next Monday.

⇒ **To make a promise or an agreement with someone:**
• I'll call you when I get to Paris.
• I'll send you the check tomorrow.

Note: Do not use "will" or "going to" in future time clauses.
SAY: As soon as you finish the report, call me and we'll review it.
NOT: As soon as you will finish the report, call me and we'll review it.

71

Quick Quiz

Form sentences from the following using "going to":

Example: The Millers / vacation in France next summer.

Answer: The Millers are going to vacation in France next summer.

1) We / rent a cottage on the beach this August.
2) What sights / show your visitors?
3) We / move to San Francisco in July.
4) I / call my doctor for an appointment.
5) Someone / fall on this slippery sidewalk.

Fill in the blanks with "going to" or "will":

1) We have squirrels in our attic. We're not sure yet what we _____ do about it.

    a) will   b) are going to

2) Nobody has taken out the trash? I _____ it.

    a) 'll do   b) 'm going to do

3) Watch out! You _____ hit the car in front of us!

    a) will   b) are going to

4) Did I tell you my plan? I _____ apply to law school.

    a) 'll   b) 'm going to

5) "Will you marry me?" — "Yes, I _____!"

    a) will   b) am going to

VISITING THE PHARMACY

Ann goes to the pharmacy to get medicine for her husband, who has a rash on his back. She talks to Ken, the pharmacist.

Ann: My husband has a rash on his back. It's **driving him nuts**.

Ken: When did the rash **break out**?

Ann: Yesterday morning. What do you think it could be?

Ken: It could be **any number of things**.

Ann: Such as?

Ken: **For starters**, it could be an **allergic reaction** to something.

Ann: I recently started using a new brand of laundry detergent. You may have **hit the nail on the head**!

Ken: If it is small red dots, it may be hives.

Ann: What do you recommend he take for it?

Ken: Is he **on** anything now?

Ann: No.

Ken: Try an **over-the-counter** anti-itch cream or a pill like Claritin.

Ann: What if those don't work? What if it gets worse?

Ken: If it doesn't **clear up**, he should see a doctor. It's probably nothing serious, but **better safe than sorry**.

Ann: Right! We should **nip this in the bud**.

IDIOMS & EXPRESSIONS

allergic reaction – sensitivity to things that come into contact with the body (causing problems such as rashes, trouble breathing, coughing, etc.)

• Irene had an **allergic reaction** to some peanuts. Her throat swelled up and she could barely breathe.

any number of things – one of many possibilities

• "What's causing my ankles to swell?" — "It could be **any number of things**."

better safe than sorry – it's good to be extra careful (to avoid trouble or disaster)

• Check the airline's website to make sure the flight hasn't been canceled. **Better safe than sorry**.

(to) break out (in) – to appear; to occur (often suddenly)

• Shortly after taking the medication, Karen **broke out** in hives.

NOTE: This is often used to describe acne that can suddenly appear on the face, especially among teenagers. Example: Emily was horrified when her face **broke out** just before the dance.

(to) clear up – to get better; to go away (when talking about problems with the skin, such as a rash or acne)

• Fortunately, Tyler's face **cleared up** before the school dance.

(to) drive one nuts – to annoy someone very much

• It **drives me nuts** when people talk during movies.

for starters – to name just one problem or example; for example

• What's wrong with Ted? **For starters**, his back is killing him.

(to) hit the nail on the head – to be right; to guess correctly

• The doctor **hit the nail on the head** when she said I needed to start exercising.

(to) nip *(this, that or it)* in the bud – to stop something before it gets any worse

• Your son has started to spend every night surfing the Web instead of doing his homework? You need to **nip that in the bud**.

---

on something – taking medication or prescription drugs

• Nancy is **on** Claritin for her allergies.

NOTE: This can also mean that one is taking illegal drugs. Example: That guy on the street corner is in bad shape. I wonder what he's **on**.

---

over-the-counter – available on the pharmacy shelf instead of by prescription

• Your headaches are getting worse? Maybe you should start taking a prescription drug instead of **over-the-counter** medications.

NOTE: sometimes you will see the abbreviation: OTC

✎ Practice the Expressions

Fill in the blanks with the missing word:

1) How long did it take for your rash to clear ____?

    a) out   b) away   c) up

2) Everything went wrong on my date with the doctor I met online. For ____, he left his wallet at home!

    a) starters   b) beginners   c) problems

3) You hit the ____ on the head when you said Tyler should get that lump on his foot checked out.

 a) screw b) tack c) nail

4) There are lots of rumors going around about why Dr. Smith is leaving her job at the clinic. We should ____ them in the bud.

 a) nip b) clip c) snip

5) All along, Jill has been taking ____-the-counter medications for her headaches, but now she's going to get a prescription.

 a) under b) over c) above

6) "What do you think this pain in my chest could be?" — "It could be ____ number of things."

 a) all b) every c) any

7) Jennifer's face broke ____ in a terrible rash.

 a) up b) out c) down

8) I have a pain in my lower back. It's ____ me nuts.

 a) bringing b) beating c) driving

9) The doctor asked Dennis how long he's been ____ Prilosec.

 a) in b) with c) on

10) Get that spot on your back checked out by a doctor. It's probably nothing, but better ____ than sorry.

 a) safe b) healthy c) well

# Language Lens: "What if"

"What if" questions are a way of asking what will happen in a certain situation. Use it to express worry or concern about a possible outcome. Note that we use the simple present form of the verb with "what if" even though we are referring to events that might happen or are possible *in the future.*

Examples:
• What if the car breaks down during our trip to California? (NOT: ~~What if the car will break down~~…)
• What if the movie is sold out by the time we get to the movie theater? (NOT: ~~What if the movie will be sold out~~…)
• What if nobody volunteers to organize the holiday party? (NOT: ~~What if nobody will volunteer~~…)
• What if somebody breaks into our house while we're on vacation? (NOT: ~~What if somebody will break~~…)
• What if I don't get into any of the law schools I applied to? (NOT: ~~What if I will not get into~~...)
• What if Angela decides to marry Pierre and move to France? (NOT: ~~What if Angela will decide~~...)

Here's what happens when you change a statement about the future into a "what if" question:

I'm worried I **won't** have enough money for college. ➔ What if I **don't** have enough money for college?

Note how the future tense verb **won't** (= will not) changes to a present tense verb (**don't**) in the "what if" question.

Here are more examples, with the verbs in bold:
• The company **will have** layoffs. ➔ What if I the company **has** layoffs?
• Erin **will get** lost on her way to your house. ➔ What if Erin **gets** lost on her way to your house?
• Nobody **will volunteer**. ➔ What if nobody **volunteers**?

Quick Quiz

I'm a "worrywart." A worrywart is someone who worries too much. Re-write my worries so I don't always have to start all my sentences with "I'm worried that." Use "What if" questions instead:

Example:
I'm worried that we won't make it to the airport on time.

Answer: What if we don't make it to the airport on time?

1) I'm worried that Joe won't get into college.

2) I'm worried that there won't be enough snow for skiing.

3) I'm worried that the restaurant will be all booked.

4) I'm worried that you won't like the movie.

5) I'm worried that our company will have layoffs next year.

6) I'm worried that the store will go out of business.

7) I'm worried that we'll run out of candy on Halloween.

8) I'm worried that our flight will be delayed.

9) I'm worried that my husband will lose his job.

10) I'm worried that our house won't sell.

VISITING THE DENTIST

Tina visits her dentist, Dr. Li, for a checkup. After taking X-rays, Dr. Li tells Tina she'll need to replace a filling.

Dr. Li: Have your teeth been **giving you any trouble** since your last **checkup**?

Tina: The back *molar* on the lower left has been **killing me**!

Dr. Li: Let's see here. It looks like the *filling* is loose.

Tina: Isn't that the same <u>one</u> you replaced last year?

Dr. Li: I'll need to check. I can't remember **off the top of my head**.

Tina: Also, <u>one</u> of my top right teeth is a little *sensitive*.

Dr. Li: Which <u>one</u>?

Tina: This <u>one</u>.

Dr. Li: Okay, I'll take a look. It looks a little *discolored*. We'll get a set of X-rays today to **get to the bottom of it**.

Tina: X-rays? Will that be an **out-of-pocket expense**?

Dr. Li: No, you're **due for** a set. It'll be **covered by** your insurance.

(Dr. Li takes the X-rays.)

Dr. Li: (looking at X-rays): Let me **give these a once over** ... It looks like we can **hold off** on that top tooth.

Tina: It does hurt, but maybe it's just a **figment of my imagination**!

Dr. Li: Call us if it keeps **acting up**. **In the meantime**, we'll need to replace that filling. Please **make an appointment** for that.

IDIOMS & EXPRESSIONS

(to) act up – to start hurting

• Rick had to stop running because his knees were **acting up**.

---

checkup – a medical examination (usually given on a regular schedule)

• Jennifer needs to call her doctor and schedule her annual **checkup**.

---

covered by – paid for by; reimbursable as part of an insurance plan

• Lisa's stay at the hospital cost $16,000. Fortunately, all of that will be **covered by** insurance.

---

due for – ready to have; time for something to happen

• "I haven't been to the eye doctor in years." — "You must be **due for** an exam."

---

figment of one's imagination – something that seems real but is not; something made up or imagined

• Was it just a **figment of my imagination**, or did our boss say he would be closing the office early tomorrow?

(to) get to the bottom of something – to find the source of a problem or issue

• My newspaper disappears from my office every day. I've got to **get to the bottom of** it.

(to) give something a once over – to look at something, often quickly

• If you have a few minutes, could you please **give my essay a once over**?

(to) give someone trouble – to hurt someone; to bother
• Ever since the car accident, Nancy's neck has been **giving her trouble**.
(to) hold off – see Lesson 1
in the meantime – until something else happens; while something else is happening
• The aspirin will make your headache go away in about half an hour. **In the meantime**, take a hot shower.
killing someone – giving someone a lot of pain; hurting badly
• Mary's stomach was **killing her**, so she left work early.
(to) make an appointment – to schedule a meeting with someone, such as a doctor, lawyer, or other specialist
• Our dog Bailey is not eating. I need to **make an appointment** with the veterinarian.
off the top of my head – from memory; without checking notes
• "Do you know Beth's email address?" — "Not **off the top of my head**. I'll need to look it up."
out-of-pocket expense – an expense that insurance does not pay for
• The dentist offers a treatment to make your teeth whiter, but it's an **out-of-pocket expense**.

✍ Practice the Expressions

Fill in the blanks with the missing word:

1) Will the dental surgery be covered _____ insurance?

   a) at   b) from   c) by

2) Ethan is due _____ a tetanus shot.

    a) at   b) for   c) with

3) Before seeing his next patient, Dr. Drake gave the woman's file a once _____.

    a) through   b) look   c) over

4) I'm afraid my front teeth are loose, but maybe it's just a figment _____ my imagination.

    a) of   b) in   c) with

5) If you feel tired all the time, you should go to the doctor and get to the bottom _____ it.

    a) with   b) of   c) in

6) In the springtime, Tanya's allergies act _____.

    a) on   b) up   c) at

7) When the receptionist asked for my insurance number, I told her I couldn't remember it _____ the top of my head.

    a) off   b) at   c) on

8) The dentist is checking your X-rays. _____ the meantime, I'll floss your teeth.

    a) During   b) At   c) In

9) My stomach is _____ me. It must have been that spicy Thai food!

    a) killing   b) aching   c) shooting

10) My knee has been _____ me trouble all week.

    a) making   b) doing   c) giving

Language Lens: One/Ones

"One" and "ones" can be used to substitute for a noun that was just mentioned.

Look at this example from the dialogue:

Dr. Li: It looks like the filling is loose.
Tina: Isn't that the same <u>one</u> you replaced last year?

Tina says "one" rather than repeating the noun (filling). She could have also said: "Isn't that the same filling you replaced last year?"

Other examples with "one":
• "Do you like the red or the blue jacket?" — "I like the red one."
• "I don't have a tie to wear to dinner." — "Let me lend you one."
• "Which ring do you like?" — "I like the one on the top shelf."
• "I'd like a chocolate chip cookie." — "We have two different kinds, one with nuts and the other without nuts. Which one do you want?"

When referring to a plural noun, use "ones."

Examples:
• "Those pastries look delicious!" — "Which ones?"
• "Please water the plants." — "Which ones?" — "The ones in the kitchen."

Look at another example from the dialogue:

Tina: Also, one of my top right teeth is a little sensitive.
Dr. Li: Which one?

You may wonder why the dentist doesn't say, "Which ones?" since "teeth" are mentioned. In this case, however, we know Tina is talking about <u>one</u> of her teeth.

Quick Quiz

Fill in the blanks with the missing word:

1) I like the blue car, but my husband prefers the green ____.

   a) one   b) ones

2) Ed offered me a glass of wine, but I told him I didn't want ____.

   a) one   b) ones

3) There's a huge pile of bottles here. Which ____ are recyclable?

   a) one   b) ones

4) "Those flowers are pretty!" — "They're the ____ I picked from the garden this morning."

   a) one   b) ones

5) "Who would like a drink?" — "I'd like ____."

   a) one   b) ones

6) I've sorted the applications into two piles. These are the applications I've already looked at, and these are the ____ I still need to review.

   a) one   b) ones

7) If you need a wedding photographer, I can recommend ____.

   a) one   b) ones

8) "Which pictures are these?" — "The ____ I took in Bali."

   a) one   b) ones

9) ____ of your friends called to ask if you're free on Saturday night, but I can't remember his name.

   a) One   b) Ones

10) ____ of Kevin's fingers is broken.

   a) One   b) Ones

AT A DINNER PARTY

Delayed by traffic, Lori and Mike arrive late to a dinner party. Their hosts, Lisa and Todd, tell them not to worry and then take their drink order.

Lori: I'm sorry we're late. We **got held up** in traffic on Route 95.

Mike: There was a **pile-up** on the highway involving three cars. A deer ran across the highway.

Lori: We were **sitting in traffic** for an hour. We <u>would've been better off</u> walking here!

Lisa: **What a nightmare!** Come on in and **chill out** now. **Join the party!**

Lori: (handing Lisa a bottle of wine): This is for you and Todd.

Lisa: Thank you.

Lori: (handing Lisa a toy car): And this is **a little something** for your son.

Lisa: Oh, how kind of you! **You shouldn't have**.

Lori: It's our pleasure.

Todd: Can I get you a drink?

Mike: A drink would **hit the spot**. What do you have?

Todd: **You name it, we've got it**.

Lori: I'll take a Bloody Mary.*

Mike: Lori, if you took Tylenol for your toothache, <u>you'd be better off</u> not drinking any alcohol!

Lori: Make that a virgin** Bloody Mary! **Hold the** vodka.

Todd: And what can I get you, Mike?

Mike: I'll take a vodka **on the rocks**.

Todd: **Coming right up!**

* Bloody Mary – a drink containing vodka, tomato juice, and usually other spices or flavorings

** A virgin drink is a mixed drink that does not include the alcohol.

IDIOMS & EXPRESSIONS

(to) chill out – to relax (especially after hard work or a bad experience)

• After taking three tests, I'm ready to just **chill out**.

Note: You can also just say "chill" without the "out."

---

coming right up – I'll bring that immediately

• One cup of coffee **coming right up**!

(to) get held up – to be delayed

• Sorry I'm late. I **got held up** in a meeting.

(to) hit the spot – to be just what one wants

• I was really hot. This iced tea really **hits the spot**!

---

hold the ____ – do not put in the ____; to not include something that would normally be part of a drink or dish

• I'll take a cheeseburger, **hold the** onions.

Join the party! – mix with the other guests

• "**Join the party!**" said Gina as we walked in the door.

(a) little something – a small gift

• I got you **a little something** for your birthday.

on the rocks – with ice (when speaking of alcoholic drinks) • Do you want your drink **on the rocks**?
pile-up – a traffic accident, usually involving many vehicles • Don't take Route 95. I just heard on the radio that there was a 25-car **pile-up** by Exit 14.
(to) sit in traffic – to be caught in traffic and unable to drive much, if at all • Don't leave Manhattan for Long Island at 4 p.m. on Friday. You'll be **sitting in traffic** for hours!
What a nightmare! – What a bad experience! • Our flight was canceled, and we ended up spending the night at the airport. **What a nightmare!**
You name it, we've got it – we have a big selection • "What drinks do you have?" — "**You name it, we've got it!**"
You shouldn't have – this is a polite way to respond when somebody gives you something • "I brought you some chocolates for your birthday." — "**You shouldn't have.**"

✎ Practice the Expressions

Choose the best substitute for the phrase or sentence in bold:

1) I'll take a Coke. **Hold the ice!**
   a) Don't put in any ice!
   b) Don't forget the ice!
   c) Make sure it's cold!

2) Let me know what you want to drink. **You name it, we've got it.**
   a) We have a few different drinks available.
   b) We have a large selection.
   c) If you tell me what you want, I'll go to the store and get it.

3) I'd like a vodka **on the rocks**.
   a) with rocks
   b) with ice
   c) with lemon juice

4) Come on in and **join the party**!
   a) talk with the other guests
   b) sign up to help at the party
   c) join our club

5) I brought **a little something** for your baby.
   a) an expensive gift
   b) a small gift
   c) a card

6) Sorry I'm late for dinner. I got **held up** at the office by an unexpected phone call.
   a) bothered
   b) disturbed
   c) delayed

7) **One cappuccino coming right up.**
   a) I'll bring you the cappuccino you asked for right away.
   b) I'll take your empty cappuccino cup away.
   c) I'll bring you the bill for one cappuccino right away.

8) Did you hear about the **pile-up** on Route 80?
   a) road construction
   b) rush hour traffic
   c) accident involving many cars

9) My wallet was stolen in Rome. **What a nightmare!**
   a) What an interesting experience!
   b) What an awful situation!
   c) What a lousy city!

10) After working hard all week, I'm ready to just **chill out**.
    a) quit my job
    b) start another project
    c) relax

# Language Lens: "Better off"

Use "better off" to:
⇒ Give advice to someone
⇒ Say what should be done

Form it like this:
would (or 'd) + be + better off + verb in -ing form

Examples:
• Your son would be better off studying in Paris instead of Lyon.
• Frank would be better off taking the train instead of the bus to Manhattan.
• You'd be better off visiting Italy in November, after all the tourists have gone.
• You'd be better off working another year before applying to business school.

⇒ **Use "would have been better off" to say what one should have done (in the past). This is sometimes used to express regret.**

Form it like this:
would have (or would've) + been + better off + verb in -ing form

---

Examples:
• We went to Spain in September, and it rained the whole time. We would have been better off going to Chile instead.
• Sharon would've been better off getting her MBA instead of a law degree.
• The fish at the Creekside Restaurant was lousy. I would've been better off ordering a hamburger.
• My college was very small. I would've been better off going to a larger school.

Quick Quiz

Practice giving advice using "You'd be better off":

Example:
Joe: Should I take a taxi or the subway to the museum?
You suggest the subway:

Answer: You'd be better off taking the subway.

1) Mark: I'm thinking of applying to business school.
You suggest law school:

2) Ashley: I'm thinking of studying abroad in Shanghai.
You suggest Beijing:

3) Ken: Should I go to India in August?
You suggest October:

4) Diane: Should I rent an apartment or buy a house?
You suggest she rent an apartment:

5) Justin: I just met Tiffany last month, but I'm thinking of asking her to marry me!
You suggest he wait:

Say what should have been done in different situations. Re-write the sentences using "would've been better off":

Example: Doug bought a house. He should have rented instead.
Answer: He would've been better off renting instead.

1) You bought a PC? You should have bought a Mac.
2) We opened an office in Russia. We should have opened an office in India instead.
3) We vacationed in Hawaii. I wish we'd gone to France instead.
4) Jim went to Princeton. He should have gone to Harvard.
5) Amber quit school to become an actress. She should have stayed in school.

MAKING INTRODUCTIONS

At the dinner party, Lisa introduces Lori and Mike to Jane and Kyle Chen. Lori and Jane realize they've met previously through work.

Lisa: Let me **make some introductions**. Lori and Mike Garcia, this is Kyle and Jane Chen.

Lori: Nice to meet you.

Kyle: I'm sorry, **I didn't catch your names**.

Lori: I'm Lori and this is my husband Mike.

Lisa: You guys **have a lot in common**, so I'm sure you'll **hit it off**.

Jane: Lori, you **look familiar**, but I **can't quite place you**.

Lori: Your name **rings a bell**. Do you work at Harco Insurance?

Jane: I <u>used to be</u> **in sales** there. I left about a year ago.

Lori: I <u>used to work</u> at Comtek International. You sold us our insurance plan.

Jane: Yes, that's right. **It's a small world!**

Lori: It sure is. I'm glad we've **crossed paths** again.

Jane: Me too. **What have you been up to** since you left Comtek?

Lori: **It's a long story**. Let's **grab some drinks**, and I'll **fill you in**.

IDIOMS & EXPRESSIONS

(to) cross paths – to meet, especially by chance

• While I was vacationing in Florida, I **crossed paths** with an old friend from high school.

(to) fill someone in (on something) – to update someone; to tell somebody what's been going on

• Can you **fill me in** on what's happening with our new business partner in China?

(to) grab some drinks – to get something to drink; to go out for a drink

• Do you want to **grab some drinks** after work?

(to) have a lot in common – to share similar interests or have similar backgrounds

• Julie and I **have a lot in common**, so we always have lots to talk about when we see each other.

(to) hit it off – to get along well with someone

• Carl **hit it off** with a woman he met on Match.com, and now they're getting married.

I can't quite place you – I've seen (or met) you before, but I can't remember where or when

• Hi, I'm Charles Kim. I know we've met before, but **I can't quite place you**.

I didn't catch your name – I didn't hear your name when you were introduced

• "I know we were introduced earlier, but **I didn't catch your name**." — "I'm Svetlana Petrenko."

NOTE: This is a polite way of asking somebody to repeat his or her name.

(to be) in sales – to work in a sales position

• Bill used to be **in sales** for Comtek, but he recently took a new job in marketing.

NOTE: You can also be **in** marketing, **in** finance, **in** real estate, **in** banking, or "in" other fields of work.

It's a long story – there's lots to say; a lot has happened; it's complicated

• "Why didn't you accept the job offer with the advertising agency?" — "**It's a long story.**"

It's a small world! – this expression is used when people are surprised to find out they know each other from some past experience

• I ran into my college friend from Chicago in a coffee shop in Vienna. **It's a small world!**

(to) look familiar – to look like someone one already knows or has seen before

• That actress **looks familiar**. Wasn't she in the movie *Midnight in Paris*?

(to) make some introductions – to introduce people

• After a few more people arrive, I'm going to **make some introductions**.

(to) ring a bell – to sound familiar; to sound like something someone has heard before

• "You graduated from Yale in 2007? Did you know Jeremy Larson?" — "No, that name doesn't **ring a bell**."

What have you been up to? – What have you been doing?

• I haven't talked to you in a long time. **What have you been up to?**

🖎 Practice the Expressions

Fill in the blanks using the following expressions:

> grab some drinks   rings a bell   paths have crossed
> fill you in   it's a long story   look familiar
> what have you been up to   it's a small world
> I can't quite place you   have a lot in common

Dan: Excuse me, haven't we met before? You __(1)__ .

Jill: Dan Reynolds?

Dan: Yes, that's me.

Jill: I'm Jill King.

Dan: Oh, that name __(2)__ , but __(3)__ .

Jill: We met at Tim Taylor's Halloween party last year.

Dan: Right! You were dressed as Cleopatra. Now here we are at Eric's party and we meet again. __(4)__ !

Jill: I'm glad our __(5)__ again.

Dan: Me too. __(6)__ ?

Jill: Not much. I thought you were going to call me after Tim's party. I remember our great discussion. As I remember, we __(7)__ .

Dan: Yes, now I remember. We both love travel and baseball!

Jill: But you never called me. What happened?

Dan: __(8)__ .

Jill: I'd love to hear it.

Dan: Let's __(9)__ and I'll __(10)__ .

94

 **Language Lens: "Used to"**

Use used to + the base form of the verb to discuss past situations, conditions, or habits which are now different or finished.
Note: "Used to" is pronounced as one word: *useta* [yooz-ta].

Examples:
• Sara used to live in New York, but now she lives in Chicago.
• Jason used to cook dinner every night, but now he gets takeout several times a week.
• Our mailman used to come at 11 a.m. every day, but now he comes later.
• Bill used to be a smoker.

⇒ With questions and negatives, the "d" on "used" is dropped.
Note: "Use to" is pronounced as one word: *useta* [yooz-ta].

Examples:
• Did you use to play football every Saturday?
• Did Jeff use to ride his bike to work?
• Susan didn't use to believe in ghosts.
• I didn't use to like apples, but now I eat one every day.

Use used to + -ing form of the verb to describe something that you are in the habit of doing.

Examples:
• I'm used to cooking dinner every night.
• I'm used to driving an hour to work.
• I'll never get used to living so far from downtown.
• We're used to sleeping in* on Sundays.

* sleep in – to sleep late on purpose (and not because you forgot to set your alarm!)

Quick Quiz

Fill in the blanks, using "used to" or "use to" + the correct verb from the list below:

get up	work	cook	want	complain
eat	arrive	wonder	dream	be

Pam __(1)__ as a lawyer for a big law firm in Manhattan. She __(2)__ at 5 a.m. every morning. She __(3)__ at the office by 7. The hours were very long. She __(4)__ sometimes why she decided to become a lawyer. She __(5)__ of becoming an actress.

Pam's husband Paul __(6)__ dinner for them every night. Pam __(7)__ dinner at 9 o'clock, when she arrived home. Every night, she complained about her job to Paul. One night, Paul asked, "Didn't you __(8)__ to be an actress?" Pam said she did. Paul suggested they move to Hollywood so Pam could pursue that old dream. Paul and Pam moved to Hollywood. Pam found work playing a lawyer on a TV show. She's much happier now. Sometimes people ask Pam, "Did you __(9)__ a lawyer? She replies, "Yes, and when I was a real lawyer, I __(10)__ a lot. Now that I play one on TV, I'm much happier!"

COMPLIMENTING A MEAL

Lori and Jane compliment Lisa on the delicious dinner she prepared. At the end of the evening, Mike and Lori thank her.

Jane: Lisa, this shrimp dish is **out of this world**!

Lori: Yes, it's delicious. You really **outdid yourself**!

Jane: You can always **count on** Lisa to serve a great meal.

Lisa: **Help yourselves** to more.

Kyle: I don't want to **make a pig of myself**.

Lisa: It's going to **go to waste** if nobody eats it.

Kyle: I'd hate to see it go to waste! I'll take a **second helping**.

Jane: Kyle, **save some room for dessert**!

Kyle: (patting large stomach): Don't worry, there's still plenty of room in here!

(two hours later)

Mike: We'd better **hit the road. Thank you for a lovely time.**

Lori: Dinner was delicious. You and Todd really **knocked yourselves out. It was a real treat.**

Lisa: It was our pleasure.

Lori: We look forward to **having you over** soon.

IDIOMS & EXPRESSIONS

(to) count on – to rely on; to depend on

• Our flight leaves at 6 a.m. tomorrow, and I'm **counting on** you to wake me up!

(to) go to waste – to be thrown out; to be wasted

• After the Thanksgiving dinner, we sent our guests home with some leftover turkey so it wouldn't **go to waste**.

(to) have someone over – to invite someone to one's house

• Sandra promised to **have us over** for dinner later this month.

(to) help oneself – to take; to serve oneself

• **Help yourself** to another piece of cake.

(to) hit the road – to leave; to get going

• We promised our babysitter we'd be home by midnight, so we'd better **hit the road** now.

It was a real treat – we had a very nice time

• Thanks for having us over for dinner. **It was a real treat**.

(to) knock oneself out – to make a big effort; to do more than necessary

• Teresa made handmade gifts for all 20 people at her office. She really **knocked herself out**.

(to) make a pig of oneself – to overeat; to eat too much

• May I have another piece of pie? I don't mean to **make a pig of myself**, but it's delicious!

out of this world – delicious

• If you go to Café Felix, be sure to order the apple pie for dessert. It's **out of this world**!

98

(to) outdo oneself – to do more than expected; to do a great job

• Danny **outdid himself** with his high school science project. He built a powerful robot.

(to) save (some) room for dessert – to not eat too much of the main course so as to be able to eat dessert

• The waitress gave us dessert menus and said, "I hope you **saved room for dessert!**"

second helping – a second portion; seconds

• There's still some lasagna left. Who'd like a **second helping**?

thank you for a lovely time – thanks for having us to your house (an expression used by guests to thank their hosts as they leave)

• "**Thank you for a lovely time**." — "Thank you for coming. It was great seeing you."

✎ Practice the Expressions

Choose the best substitute for the phrase or sentence in bold:

1) This lamb dish is **out of this world**.
   a) pretty good
   b) not bad
   c) delicious

2) Would anybody like **a second helping**?
   a) more food
   b) some help
   c) some dessert

3) It's already 11 o'clock? We should **hit the road**.
   a) make some plans
   b) go to sleep
   c) leave

4) Spending the weekend at Tina's summer home was **a real treat**.
   a) boring
   b) tiring
   c) enjoyable

5) The bride's mother did all the cooking for the wedding. She really **outdid herself**.
   a) exhausted herself
   b) did a great job
   c) did better than she usually does

6) Thanks for inviting us over for dinner next Saturday. Please don't **knock yourselves out**.
   a) do a lot of work
   b) serve us anything good
   c) serve us more than we can eat

7) We'd like to **have you over** soon.
   a) come to your house
   b) invite you to our house
   c) go out with you

8) If that last piece of fish is going to **go to waste**, I'll take it.
   a) get eaten by somebody else
   b) get thrown back into the sea
   c) get thrown in the garbage

9) **Save room for dessert**. I made apple pie.
   a) Don't eat so much that you're too full to have dessert.
   b) Make space available on your plate.
   c) Don't eat too much dessert.

10) Please **help yourselves to** more cookies.
    a) save
    b) take
    c) make

Language Lens: Reflexive Pronouns

Use a reflexive pronoun when the subject and the object of the sentence or clause are the same. In other words, the subject of the sentence or clause does something *to itself* or *for itself.*

These are the reflexive pronouns:

Singular:
me – myself
you– yourself
he – himself
she – herself
it – itself
one – oneself

Plural:
we – ourselves
you – yourselves
they – themselves

Compare when to use a reflexive pronoun with when to use a regular pronoun:

⇒ **Reflexive pronoun:** the subject and object are <u>the same person</u>

Lisa bought Lisa a present. ➔ Lisa bought **herself** a present.
(subject)   (object)

⇒ **Regular pronoun:** the subject and object are <u>different people</u>

Lisa bought Larry a present. ➔ Lisa bought **him** a present.
(subject)   (object)

Expressions with -self / -selves

Here are some common expressions with reflexive pronouns:
- behave oneself: I hope the baby will behave herself at the restaurant.
- by oneself – note the two different meanings:
    1: alone. Tim has no plans for Easter. He'll be home by himself.
    2: without help. Billy can tie his shoes by himself!
- cut oneself: I cut myself while chopping onions.
- enjoy oneself: Enjoy yourselves on your trip to China!
- hurt oneself: Isabella hurt herself at the playground.
- look at oneself: Look at yourself in the mirror.
- tell oneself: Tiffany told herself everything would be okay.
- kill oneself: Joel is killing himself by working 100 hours a week.

Reflexive pronouns can also be used for emphasis:
- Now you want me to go to the training program? Yesterday you yourself said it would be a waste of time!
- Our boss made us work on Christmas day. He himself took the day off.
- These cookies are delicious! Did you make them yourself?
- You don't have time to fix my computer? Then I'll do it myself!

Note: Do not assume that if a verb takes a reflexive form in your native language, it is also reflexive in English.

Warning: The reflexive pronoun "myself" is often used incorrectly. People use it instead of the pronouns "me" or "I." You'll even hear native speakers make this mistake. Here are a couple of examples of what to say and what not to say:

SAY: Please give the book to Paul or me.
NOT: ~~Please give the book to Paul or myself.~~

SAY: Either Evan or I will give the speech.
NOT: ~~Either Evan or myself will give the speech.~~

Quick Quiz

Fill in the blanks with the missing word:

1) Sara and Sam, help _____ to more pie!

   a) yourself   b) yourselves   c) myself

2) I hope you're not going to be by _____ on your birthday.

   a) yourselves   b) yourself   c) myself

3) Don't call a plumber to fix the sink. Fix it _____!

   a) himself   b) yourself   c) myself

4) Ouch! I cut _____ while slicing a tomato.

   a) himself   b) yourself   c) myself

5) Did your daughter write that wonderful story all by _____?

   a) itself   b) herself   c) oneself

6) Troy and Melissa taught _____ Spanish.

   a) herself   b) theirselves   c) themselves

7) Brian ate the entire pie? He needs to learn to control _____!

   a) herself   b) itself   c) himself

8) I made this Christmas ornament _____.

   a) itself   b) myself   c) yourself

9) That's strange. The light just turned on by _____.

   a) himself   b) herself   c) itself

10) You forgot to make dinner reservations? Never mind. I'll do it _____.

   a) myself   b) yourself   c) itself

There are lots of other people here in the same boat.

HANDLING A DELAY AT THE AIRPORT

Tom's flight to Chicago on Flyaway Airlines has been delayed, and now he worries he'll miss his meeting. He talks to Mike, a representative of the airline.

VOICE: Attention passengers on Flight 394 to Chicago. This flight has been delayed. Please **stand by** for more information.

Tom: Excuse me, I'm on the flight to Chicago. When will it depart now?

Mike: It looks like it'll be delayed at least two hours. I'll **keep you posted**.

Tom: I have a 4 o'clock meeting in Chicago. If the flight gets in at 3:30, there's **no way** I'll make it.

Mike: Sorry, but there's nothing I can do. There are lots of other people here **in the same boat**.

Tom: Are there any other flights to Chicago?

Mike: Yes, there's a 1 p.m. departure, but it's **fully booked**.

Tom: Can you **put me on the waiting list**?

Mike: I'll add you to the list, but **don't hold your breath**. There are **quite a few** people already on the list.

Tom: Can I fly another airline?

Mike: Other airlines won't **honor your Flyaway Airlines ticket**.

Tom: Oh, **for crying out loud**! This is so <u>annoying</u>.

Mike: I'm sorry you're <u>annoyed</u>, but there's nothing more I can do.

Tom: Let me **give you a piece of my mind**. I won't be using Flyaway Airlines again anytime soon!

IDIOMS & EXPRESSIONS

don't hold your breath – don't count on it; it's unlikely

• Becky said she'd invite us over for dinner this week, but **don't hold your breath**. She's unreliable.

for crying out loud – an expression one says when annoyed or angry

• **For crying out loud**! Somebody parked right behind us in the parking lot, and now we can't get our car out!

fully booked – having no availability; with all seats taken

• I wanted to take an 8 a.m. flight from New York to London, but the flight was **fully booked**.

(to) give someone a piece of one's mind – to tell someone what one really thinks

• Our waiter has been really slow all evening. I'm going to **give him a piece of my mind**!

(to) honor a ticket – to accept a ticket

• Since Delta Airlines canceled my flight to Orlando, they promised that another airline would **honor my ticket**.

in the same boat – in the same bad situation; sharing the same negative experience

• When the airport shut down due to a blizzard, I was stuck in the airport. Many other people were **in the same boat**.

(to) keep someone posted – to update someone; to give someone the latest information

• **Keep me posted** on your flight status.

no way – no chance

• The report is due on Friday? There's **no way** we're going to finish it on time.

put someone on a *(or the)* waiting list – to add somebody to a list of people waiting for a service

• You want to upgrade to business class? I'll **put you on the waiting list**.

quite a few – many; a fairly large number

• **Quite a few** passengers were stuck at Kennedy Airport overnight after their flights were canceled due to bad weather.

(to) stand by – to wait for further information

• Passengers for Flight 52 to Dallas, your flight has been delayed. Please **stand by**.

✍ Practice the Expressions

Choose the best substitute for the phrase or sentence in bold:

1) We lost our power in the snowstorm. Our neighbors' houses were also dark, so we knew they were **in the same boat**.
   a) traveling with us
   b) in the same situation
   c) on vacation

2) **For crying out loud!** We've been sitting here for 20 minutes waiting for the waiter to come take our order.
   a) Let's speak up!
   b) Good news!
   c) How annoying!

3) Maria's Bistro is **fully booked** for tonight.
   a) available
   b) not available
   c) closed

4) You're going out on a date with the guy you met on the Internet? Good luck and **keep me posted**!
   a) tell me what happens
   b) call me while you're on the date
   c) be careful

5) Sorry, we can't **honor your bus tickets**. They're for a different bus company.
   a) accept your bus tickets
   b) refund your bus tickets
   c) return your bus tickets

6) We got to Costco before the store opened. There were **quite a few** people waiting in line to get in.
   a) one or two
   b) thousands of
   c) many

7) Adam said he's going to invite us to his cottage this summer, but **don't hold your breath**.
   a) don't talk to him about it
   b) don't accept his invitation
   c) don't count on it

8) Look at this traffic! There's **no way** we'll be on time for the play.
   a) a possibility
   b) no chance
   c) some chance

9) Please **stand by** for more information.
   a) ask
   b) stand over there
   c) wait

10) Your doctor failed to diagnose your illness and now it's worse? You should call him and **give him a piece of your mind**.
   a) tell him you're angry because he made a mistake
   b) offer to let him examine your head
   c) ask him if you can come in for another examination

Language Lens: Annoyed/Annoying

"Annoying" describes the person, place, or thing that **causes** one's feelings. "Annoyed" says **how** one feels. Something is annoying, so one feels annoyed. Remember: the cause of the feelings ends in -ing. The way one feels ends in -ed. Here's a list of other word pairs that follow the same pattern:

Cause of the feelings	How one feels
Something is...	*...so one feels*
surprising	surprised
boring	bored
interesting	interested
disappointing	disappointed
amazing	amazed
confusing	confused
exciting	excited
exhausting	exhausted
terrifying	terrified
shocking	shocked
irritating	irritated
horrifying	horrified
energizing	energized

Examples:
• That was an exhausting trip. I feel exhausted!
• What shocking news! I'm shocked.
• The lecture was boring. I was so bored I almost fell asleep.
• These driving directions are confusing. I'm confused.
• The massage was energizing. I felt energized afterwards.
• This is exciting news! I'm so excited.

Quick Quiz

Fill in the blanks with the missing word:

1) After traveling around China for three weeks on business, Chad is ____.

   a) exhausting   b) exhausted

2) It's ____ when people talk during movies.

   a) annoyed   b) annoying

3) You're getting married in July? How ____!

   a) exciting   b) excited

4) That's ____ that your daughter can already say the alphabet at just 18 months!

   a) amazed   b) amazing

5) I was ____ when my friend called and said she couldn't come visit for the weekend.

   a) disappointing   b) disappointed

6) Nate is ____ in other cultures, so he'd make a good diplomat.

   a) interested   b) interesting

7) No wonder people fall asleep in Professor Martin's class. He's so ____.

   a) boring   b) bored

8) Pat found the documentary on Thomas Jefferson very ____.

   a) interested   b) interesting

9) Dana didn't call you to wish you a happy birthday? That's ____.

   a) surprised   b) surprising

10) The instructions are ____. I can't figure out how to install this new software.

   a) confusing   b) confused

DEALING WITH LOST LUGGAGE

Tom complains to Jim, a Flyaway Airlines representative, that his suitcase is lost. Jim asks him to fill out some paperwork and assures him his bag will likely be found.

Tom: Excuse me, I just arrived on the flight from Atlanta and my suitcase is missing.

Jim: Did you wait until all the bags were *unloaded*?

Tom: Yes, I did. My suitcase is not there.

Jim: Here's a card with various suitcases. Which looks most like your piece of luggage?

Tom: It's like this one, and it's green.

Jim: Okay, I'll just have you **fill out this paperwork**.

Tom: I had all my clothes for a meeting this afternoon in that bag. Now I'm **in a bind**.

Jim: We'll *reimburse* you for clothing you buy today for up to $100.

Tom: I'm really **pressed for time**. I won't have time to go shopping for a new suit now!

Jim: Well, we'll **do our best** to **track down** your bag as quickly as possible.

Tom: What if my suitcase is lost **for good**?

Jim: Baggage usually **turns up**, so **let's cross that bridge when we come to it**.

Tom: I'm really **up the creek** now. **It boggles my mind** how you can just lose someone's luggage!

Jim: Let me give you <u>a piece of advice</u>. Next time, wear your suit on the airplane.

Tom: Thanks for the <u>advice</u>. Next time I think I'll fly a different airline!

IDIOMS & EXPRESSIONS

(to) do one's best – to try hard

• I'll **do my best** to finish the report by Friday.

(to) fill out paperwork – to complete one or more forms

• Before seeing the doctor, you'll need to **fill out this paperwork**.

---

for good – forever; permanently

• After graduating from college, Ryan moved back in with his parents. They hope he'll move out **for good** soon.

---

in a bind – in a difficult situation; in need of help

• Our school is **in a bind**. We need $10,000 to buy new textbooks, but there's no money in our budget for it.

---

it (or that) boggles my mind – I'm very surprised by that

• Some people spend $100 a day to send their dogs to a spa. **That boggles my mind!**

---

let's cross that bridge when we come to it – let's not worry about that until we need to

• "What if we can't find a buyer for our house?" — **"Let's cross that bridge when we come to it."**

pressed for time – in a hurry; not having much time

• We asked the waiter to bring the check with dinner, explaining that we were **pressed for time**.

(to) track down – to find (often after a long search)

• A Picasso was stolen from the Metropolitan Museum? I hope they can **track down** the thieves!

(to) turn up – to be found

• Angela hopes her missing earring will **turn up** before the dance on Saturday.

up the creek – in trouble; in a very difficult situation

• Our rent is due on Friday, and we have no money in our bank account. We're **up the creek**!

NOTE: The longer form of this expression is: up the creek without a paddle.

✎ Practice the Expressions

Fill in the blanks with the missing word:

1) The CEO of Walt Disney made over $53 million last year. That boggles my _____!

   a) brain   b) mind   c) head

2) I can't find my theater ticket anywhere. Can you help me track it _____?

   a) up   b) over   c) down

3) Can I call you back later? I'm pressed _____ time right now.

   a) with   b) in   c) for

4) Good news! My missing theater ticket just turned ____.

   a) down   b) up   c) in

5) Ted needs to be at the airport in an hour and his car won't start. He's ____ a bind.

   a) up   b) with   c) in

6) Is Paul moving to Prague for ____ or is he just going to spend a year or two there?

   a) better   b) best   c) good

7) "What if we can't get up our driveway due to the snowstorm?" — "Let's cross that ____ when we come to it."

   a) street   b) river   c) bridge

8) If you want to apply for a job with the Central Intelligence Agency, be prepared to fill ____ a lot of paperwork.

   a) in   b) out   c) up

9) If we don't get our visas for Vietnam by next Tuesday, we're going to be up the ____.

   a) creek   b) river   c) stream

10) ____ your best to finish your homework so you can come to the movies with us.

   a) Make   b) Have   c) Do

Language Lens: Count & Non-count Nouns

Count nouns (also called "countable nouns") are people, places, or things that <u>we can count</u>. They can be singular *(a chair, a cup, a cat)* or plural *(chairs, cups, cats)*.

Non-count nouns are materials, substances, concepts, information, etc. which <u>we cannot count</u>.

Here are some common non-count nouns:		
accommodation	furniture	postage
advice	garbage	progress
air	homework	research
baggage	information	software
bread	knowledge	sugar
butter	love	traffic
clothing	luggage	trouble
equipment	money	water
energy	music	weather
fruit	news	work

Non-count nouns:

⇒ We do not use "a/an" directly before non-count nouns. To express a quantity of one of these nouns, use a word or phrase like:
- a piece of: a piece of bread, a piece of advice, a piece of news
- a cup of: a cup of soup, a cup of water, a cup of tea
- some: some information, some news, some furniture
- a lot of: a lot of water, a lot of luggage, a lot of happiness

⇒ Non-count nouns are always singular. Remembering this can help you avoid a lot of mistakes.

Say: This is good news! NOT: ~~These are good news!~~
Say: The equipment is heavy. NOT: ~~The equipment are heavy.~~
Say: The information is valuable. NOT: ~~The information are valuable.~~
Say: My luggage is heavy. NOT: ~~My luggage are heavy.~~
Say: The money is in the bank. NOT: ~~The money are in the bank.~~

Count nouns:

⇒ A <u>singular</u> count noun always takes either the indefinite article (a, an) or the definite article (the):

• Tracy is looking for **a job**.
• Did Tracy get **the job** she applied for?

⇒ A <u>plural</u> count noun takes the definite article (the) if it refers to a definite, **specific** group. It takes no article if used in a **general** sense (generalizations):

• **The dogs** you adopted are cute. (specific → the)
• **Dogs** are fun pets. (general → no article)

Using the quantity expressions much, many, a little, a few:

Much/Many
⇒ Use **much** with non-count nouns:
• How much change should we bring?
• I wish you much happiness. (I wish you a lot of happiness).*

⇒ Use **many** with count nouns:
• How many quarters should we bring?
• I took many great classes. (I took a lot of great classes).*

* Note: In statements like these, you can also use "a lot of" instead of "much" or "many." It sounds more conversational.

Little/A Few
⇒ Use **little** with non-count nouns:
• We have made little progress since the summer.
• Sam has little money left.

⇒ Use **few** with count nouns:
• We have completed a few projects since the summer.
• Sam has a few dollars left.

Quick Quiz

Fill in the blanks with the missing word or words:

1) Let me give you _____.
   a) an advice   b) a piece of advice

2) _____ good news!
   a) This is   b) These are

3) We are making _____ with our report.
   a) a progress   b) progress

4) Neil has _____ friends.
   a) many   b) much

5) I wish you _____ luck with your job search.
   a) many   b) much

6) The information you gave me _____ useful.
   a) are   b) is

7) The clothing you gave my daughter_____ beautiful.
   a) are   b) is

8) We had _____ time for sightseeing on our business trip.
   a) few   b) little

9) I only have _____ dollars left in my wallet.
   a) a few   b) a little

10) How _____ cups of coffee have you had today?
   a) much   b) many

Nine bucks a gallon? That's highway robbery!

RENTING A CAR

Peter talks to Sam at the rental car counter about renting a car. Sam tells Peter about a special offer they're having and helps him understand how the rental fees work.

Sam: Hello. How can I help you?

Peter: I'd like to rent a car for the weekend.

Sam: What size did you **have in mind**?

Peter: I'd like your cheapest car, so I guess that would be a *compact*.

Sam: We're **running a special** right now. You can rent a mid-size car for the same price as a compact. It's $55 a day **inclusive of** tax, plus insurance. It's <u>such</u> a great deal!

Peter: Okay, I'll take it.

Sam: All right. Let me just print out the agreement … Here you go, **read that over**, please.

Peter: I **can't make heads or tails of** this information. Do I really need insurance? I already have a good auto insurance plan.

Sam: Then you're probably **all set**. I do recommend the collision damage waiver.* It's only $10 a day. That way, if you **bang up** the car, you won't owe us anything.

Peter: I'm sure I won't have an accident, but I'll take it **just in case**.

Sam: Very good. If you don't return the car with a full tank of gas, we charge $9 a gallon to refill it.

Peter: Nine bucks a gallon? That's <u>so</u> expensive. It's **highway robbery**!

Sam: Be sure to return the car by 5 p.m. on Sunday.

Peter: Five? That's going to be **cutting it close**. The conference I'm attending ends at 4:30. What if I get it here at 6 on Sunday?

Sam: It'll be another $65.

Peter: There's no **grace period**?

Sam: There's a 29 minute **grace period**. So you could return the car at 5:29 and still be okay.

Peter: Okay, thanks. You've been <u>such</u> a big help.

Sam: You're very welcome. Here's the key. The car is in space A4. You're **good to go**.

* collision damage waiver – with this optional coverage, the car rental company cannot hold the customer responsible for any damage to the car

IDIOMS & EXPRESSIONS

all set – see Lesson 6

(to) bang up – (to) damage

• Right after Tyler got his driver's license, he borrowed his mother's car and **banged it up**.

(to) cut it close – (to) not leave enough time to get somewhere or to do something

• The play starts at 8:00, and you're planning to leave the house at 7:30? That's **cutting it close**.

good to go – ready to go; taken care of; prepared

• We've got our tents, our flashlights, and our food. We're **good to go**!

grace period – a period after a deadline in which additional fees are <u>not</u> charged

• My credit card payment is due by the 15th of the month. But there's a 2-day **grace period**.

(to) have in mind – to be thinking about as a possibility

• "You're offering me $2,500 for the car? That's so little!" — "What did you **have in mind**?"

highway robbery – very overpriced; a fee that is too high

• I really wanted a cup of coffee at the airport, but the coffee shop was charging $4 a cup. That's **highway robbery**!

inclusive of – including; already included in the amount

• The cost of the car repairs is going to be $350, **inclusive of** parts and labor.

just in case – if something happens; because there is a small chance that (something could happen)

• I don't think it'll rain today, but you should take your umbrella **just in case**.

(to) not be able to make heads or tails of – to be unable to interpret

• This apartment rental contract is so confusing. I **can't make heads or tails of** it.

(to) read over – to review; to take a look at, often with the goal of making edits or making sure everything is okay

• I'd appreciate it if you'd **read over** my résumé.

(to) run a special – to offer lower prices on something, for a certain period of time

• The clothing store is **running a special** this week. Buy one shirt and get the second at half price.

✎ Practice the Expressions

Fill in the blanks with the missing word:

1) The weather forecast calls for sunny skies for the entire week we're in Italy. But I'm bringing along a raincoat just in _____.
   a) case   b) cause   c) careful

2) You want a new job title? What did you have in _____?
   a) head   b) ideas   c) mind

3) Fifteen dollars for a sandwich? That's _____ robbery!
   a) roadside   b) motorway   c) highway

4) You're leaving your house at 5:30 for a 7 o'clock flight? That's cutting it _____.
   a) sharp   b) close   c) near

5) Would you mind reading _____ my business school essays?
   a) over   b) on   c) upon

6) Sorry, the grace _____ is over. We're going to have to charge you interest on your account.
   a) phase   b) time   c) period

7) Tom wrote me a note, but I can't make heads or _____ of it. His handwriting is so messy!
   a) tails   b) feet   c) sense

8) We got our visas for Brazil. We're good to _____.
   a) leave   b) go   c) be

9) The airfare to Seoul is $1500, inclusive _____ taxes.
   a) with   b) of   c) by

10) How did you bang _____ your car?
    a) up   b) down   c) on

Language Lens: So and Such

So and **such** are both used to express extremes. They are often used in exclamations (and they are *so* useful!).

So
⇒ Use "so" before an adjective (without a noun)
⇒ Use "so" before an adverb

Examples with so:
- Andy is so good at tennis! NOT: ~~Andy is so good tennis player!~~
- Angela's baby is so cute!
- Jay's new painting is so beautiful. He's so talented!
- Your house is so beautiful.
- That was so kind of you!
- John works so hard.
- Kristen looked so lovely in her wedding dress.

Such
⇒ Use "such" before an adjective + noun
⇒ Use "such" before a noun

Note that when the noun is singular, "a" or "an" comes after "such."

Examples with such:
- That was such a scary movie! NOT: ~~That was so scary movie!~~
- That's such a cute baby!
- You are such a good friend.
- Phil is such a hard worker.
- You prepared such a delicious meal.
- This project is such a headache!
- Why do you carry such heavy bags?

Quick Quiz

Fill in the blanks with the missing word:

1) Emily is _____ a nice girl. I love babysitting for her.
     a) so   b) such

2) The movie was _____ boring that I could barely stay awake.
     a) so   b) such

3) The flight was _____ long that I thought we'd never get there.
     a) so   b) such

4) If you study for it, the TOEFL is not _____ a difficult exam.
     a) so   b) such

5) People in our office leave leftovers in the refrigerator for months. It's _____ gross!
     a) so   b) such

6) Nora hasn't been to the dentist in _____ a long time.
     a) so   b) such

7) Canyon Ranch is a great spa, but it's _____ expensive!
     a) so   b) such

8) You did _____ a great job on your presentation!
     a) so   b) such

9) Tina's boss keeps criticizing her. Why is he being _____ nasty?
     a) so   b) such

10) You got promoted? That's _____ good news!
     a) so   b) such

CHECKING IN TO A HOTEL

When Maria goes to check in to her hotel, Chad, at reception, informs her that he doesn't have her reservation. He finds a room for her, which ends up being too noisy.

Chad:　How can I help you?

Maria:　I'm **checking in**. I've got a reservation under the name Baker.

Chad:　Okay, let me **pull up your reservation**. You said "Baker."

Maria:　Yes, Maria Baker.

Chad:　Unfortunately, I have no record of your reservation. It <u>must have gotten</u> lost in our system.

Maria:　Great. **Just my luck!**

Chad:　Don't worry. We've got plenty of rooms. Are you a member of our **rewards program** yet?

Maria:　No, I don't travel that much so it's not **worth my while**.

Chad:　You can start **earning points** with this stay. Then you can get discounts on future stays and **special offers** by mail.

Maria:　**As a rule**, I don't join those programs. I get enough **junk mail** already.

(ten minutes later)

Maria:　I just checked my room, and I'll need a different room.

Chad: What's the problem?

Maria: The 12th floor is a **zoo**. There's some kind of *convention* going on up there and people are **making a racket**.

Chad: I'm sorry about that. Let's see what else we have.

Maria: Also, you <u>must have given</u> me a smoking room because it **reeks of** cigarette smoke!

Chad: **I do apologize for that**. Let me give you room 1485. It should be quiet and smoke free.

IDIOMS & EXPRESSIONS

as a rule – in general; usually

• **As a rule**, Betty doesn't answer her telephone after 10 p.m.

(to) check in – to register (such as at a hotel or conference)

• Let's **check in** to our hotel first, and then go out and explore the city.

(to) earn points – to earn credit towards a future purchase (when talking about promotions offered by companies)

• Allison joined Delta's frequent flier program and started **earning points**.

I do apologize (for that) – I'm very sorry (said to a customer)

• Your order arrived a week late? **I do apologize for that**.

Note: The "do" in this expression is optional. It makes the apology stronger or more polite.

---

junk mail – unwanted mail, usually selling or advertising something

• My mailbox was full today, but it was almost all **junk mail**.

just my luck – what bad luck

• I arrived two minutes late to the airport and missed my flight. **Just my luck!**

(to) make a racket – to make a lot of noise

• We couldn't sleep because the people in the hotel room next door were **making a racket** all night.

(to) pull up a reservation – to find a reservation on the computer; to call up the file with the reservation

• "Hello, I'd like to change my flight for next Friday." — "Please give me your last name and I'll **pull up our reservation**."

(to) reek of – to smell badly of something (often smoke or alcohol)

• This pillow **reeks of** smoke. Please bring me a fresh one.

rewards program – a promotional program designed to get customers to use a company's product or service more often

• Paula earned a free one-week stay at a Marriott through the hotel's **rewards program**.

special offer – a promotional offer; a discount on a particular product or service, usually for a limited time

• The restaurant is running a **special offer**. Buy one meal at full price and get the second one free.

worth one's while – deserving of one's time or effort

• If you're in Manhattan, I suggest you visit the Guggenheim Museum. It'll be **worth your while**.

zoo – a noisy area; chaos

• Thousands of people go to Times Square in New York to celebrate New Year's Eve. It's a **zoo!**

✎ Practice the Expressions

Fill in the blanks using the following expressions:

worth my while	just our luck	reeked of
made a racket	as a rule	rewards program
special offers	earn points	check in zoo

Two years ago, I decided to join the Continental Hotel's (1) .
I figured it would be (2) since I travel frequently on business.
Whenever I stay at a Continental Hotel, I (3) . They also send me
 (4) in the mail.

Last week, my husband and I decided to use the points and spend
the weekend in Manhattan. (5) , we only travel when we can get
a special deal.

When we arrived to (6) , the hotel was a (7) . It turns out that
some company was having its annual sales conference there that
weekend. (8) ! The attendees (9) all weekend, partying both
nights until 3 a.m. The hallways (10) cigarette smoke. We didn't
get much sleep, but we did enjoy sightseeing in the city.

Language Lens: "Must have"

To say what you **think** has happened in a situation, use *must have* or the contraction *must've.*

Form it like this:

must have (or must've) + verb in the past participle

The past participle of regular verbs usually ends in -ed. It is the same as the verb in the past tense. *Examples:* visited, looked, entered, wanted. Irregular verbs have various endings in the past participle. Most end in one of these:
-d (heard, held, paid, read, stood, understood)
-n (eaten, forgotten, given, gotten, known, taken, spoken)
-t (brought, caught, cost, left, slept, spent, thought)

Examples:
• I can't find my passport. I must've* left it at the hotel. *(= I think I left it at the hotel).*
• You don't have your book? You must have forgotten it in my car.
• The movie is over already? I must've fallen asleep.
• I can't find my laptop. Someone must've moved it.
• Linda called you from her car saying she was lost? She must've left the directions at home.
• My stomach is killing me. I must've overeaten!
• My iPad is gone from my hotel room. Someone must've stolen it!
• There are no more cookies left? Kate must've eaten the last one.

* Note: must've can be pronounced either *mustof* or, more informally, *musta.*

Quick Quiz

Say what you think happened in each situation. Put the verb in parentheses into the correct form with "must've":

Example:
We're lost. We _____ (take) a wrong turn somewhere.

Answer: We <u>must've taken</u> a wrong turn somewhere.

1) The radio isn't working anymore. It _____ (ran) out of batteries.

2) It's dark in the house. Somebody _____ (turn) out all the lights.

3) You have big bags under your eyes. You _____ (stay) up all night.

4) Maya's doll is missing its arms. She _____ (pull) them off.

5) You're all wet. You _____ (forget) your umbrella!

6) My laptop is missing from my office. Somebody _____ (steal) it!

7) I can't find my glasses. I _____ (leave) them at the office.

8) You got here in less than an hour. You _____ (drive) fast!

9) It's already 10 a.m. I _____ (oversleep).

10) Your French is fluent. You _____ (study) it in school.

TRAVELING BY CAR

Sara and Nick are taking a car trip. Nick has taken a wrong turn, and now they need to stop and ask for directions.

Sara: Do you think we can make it to Joe and Mary's by 7?

Nick: <u>I hope so</u>. It's only 5 o'clock now and we've only got about 120 miles left to go. We're **making good time**.

Sara: Yes, but we still need to **make a pit stop**. Don't you want to stop somewhere and **grab a bite**?

Nick: <u>I guess so</u>. Let's look for a place we can **turn off**.

Sara: I just saw a sign that said Route 584 North. Aren't we supposed to be on 80 East!

Nick: Yes. We must've **taken a wrong turn** somewhere.

Sara: I thought you said you **knew these roads like the back of your hand**. Did you **doze off** or what?

Nick: We'd better stop at a gas station and ask for directions.

(at the gas station)

Sara: Hi, we're lost. Can you tell me the quickest way to get on 80 East?

Clerk: **Hang a left** out of the gas station. **Hop on** 35 South. Take it about 10 miles and you'll see a sign for 80 East.

Sara: Thanks a lot.

(back in the car)

Nick: Did you get the directions?

Sara: Yes. Left out of here, then 35 South to 80 East.

Nick: **Got it**.

Sara: Careful! You almost hit a piece of tire in the road.

Nick: Please don't be a **backseat driver**!

Sara: I try to **bite my tongue**, but sometimes **I can't help myself**.

IDIOMS & EXPRESSIONS

backseat driver – a passenger who offers unwanted driving advice

• "You're driving too close to the car in front of us." — "Don't be a **backseat driver!**"

(to) bite one's tongue – to not say what one is really thinking; to resist saying something one wants to say

• Mary doesn't like her husband's snacking habits, but she tries to **bite her tongue**.

(to) doze off – to fall asleep

• Matt stayed up so late doing his homework, he ended up **dozing off** in class.

got it – I understand; do you understand

• "Take a right at the light and go three blocks. The restaurant will be on your right." — "**Got it**."
• "You can borrow my car, but bring it back by 9. **Got it**?" — "**Got it**."

(to) grab a bite – to get something quick to eat

• Let's meet at 7 o'clock and **grab a bite** before the concert.

(to) hang a left / a right – to turn left / right

• **Hang a right** at the next stoplight and you'll see the Whole Foods on your right.

(to) hop on – to get on a road

• If you're going downtown, **hop on** the highway. It's the fastest way.

I can't help myself – I can't stop myself; I can't resist

• "Stop telling me how to drive!" — "Sorry, **I can't help myself**."

(to) know something like the back of one's hand – to know very well (said most often about streets or places)

• We don't need to bring a map with us. I **know Boston like the back of my hand**.

(to) make a pit stop – to make a quick stop, usually to use the bathroom or to get something to eat

• "Would you mind **making a pit stop**? After drinking so much coffee, I need to use the bathroom."

(to) make good time – to travel efficiently; to get somewhere in less time than expected

• It's noon and we're already in Pennsylvania? We're **making good time**!

(to) take a wrong turn – to turn where one shouldn't have

• We were headed to Manhattan, but we **took a wrong turn** and ended up in Brooklyn.

(to) turn off – to exit the highway

• I think we're going the wrong way. **Turn off** here and we'll check the map.

✎ Practice the Expressions

Fill in the blanks using the following expressions:

> grab a bite   taken a wrong turn   doze off
>
>   turn off   like the back of your hand
>
> backseat driver   made a pit stop   bite my tongue
>
>   making good time   I can't help myself

Doug: I just saw a sign that said "Entering New York." We must have   (1)   somewhere.

Lynn: Oh no! You told me you knew these roads   (2) .

Doug: I thought I did.

Lynn: I'm getting hungry anyway. Let's stop somewhere to   (3) , and we can ask for directions.

Doug: Yeah, I'd better get some coffee so I don't   (4) . We haven't   (5)   in a few hours.

Lynn: Let's   (6)   at the next exit and look for a restaurant.

Doug: I can't believe we're going the wrong way. I thought we were   (7) . Now we're going to be late.

Lynn: Hey, slow down! We don't want to miss the exit.

Doug: Please don't be a   (8) .

Lynn: Sorry, sometimes   (9) , but I'll try to   (10) in the future!

Language Lens: Phrases with "so"

To give a positive reply, use "so" instead of "yes" after: afraid, believe, guess, hope, suppose, and think.

Say	Do NOT Say
I'm afraid so	~~I'm afraid yes~~
I believe so	~~I believe yes~~
I guess so	~~I guess yes~~
I hope so	~~I hope yes~~
I think so	~~I think yes~~
I suppose so	~~I suppose yes~~

"I'm afraid so" means "unfortunately, yes."

Say "I guess so" or "I suppose so" to mean you are not too happy about doing something.

Examples:
• "Did your team lose?" — "I'm afraid so."
• "Do we have next Monday off?" — "I believe so."
• "Should we invite Brad to the party?" — "I guess so."
• "Don't you think we'll have good weather?" — "I hope so."
• "Will it snow tonight?" — "I think so."
• "Can I borrow the car on Friday night?" — "I suppose so."

Quick Quiz

Give a positive reply to the following, using the verb in parentheses + so:

Example:
1) Is John coming home for Thanksgiving? (hope)

Answer: I hope so.

1) Are Ken and Tanya going to get married? (hope)

2) Are you going to Ivan's party on Saturday night? (think)

3) Did you forget to water the plants while I was away? (afraid)

4) Do you think we should take a taxi downtown? (guess)

5) Are they serving dinner at the holiday party? (think)

6) Did somebody drink the last can of Diet Coke? (afraid)

7) Are we getting off work early this Friday? (hope)

8) Can you loan me your iPod? (guess)

9) Is Keith going to get promoted? (think)

10) Is David joining us for dinner on Saturday? (hope)

Lesson 21

TAKING A TAXI

Ian gets in a taxi. He's in a big rush because he has an interview in 10 minutes. Unfortunately, he gets stuck in traffic.

Ali: **Where are you headed?**

Ian: 411 Wall Street.

Ali: **Hop in!**

Ian: I've got a meeting in 10 minutes. Can you **step on it**?

Ali: This is the <u>fastest</u> I can go. If I go any <u>faster</u>, I'm going to **get pulled over**.

Ian: Don't you know some **back roads** we can take?

Ali: No, this is the <u>best</u> way to go. Oops! That was a **close call**. That bus almost hit us!

Ian: I've got an interview at 10.

Ali: I hate to **break it to** you, but there's **bumper-to-bumper traffic up ahead**.

Ian: Yes, I see that **traffic is heavy**. What's going on?

Ali: It looks like there was a **fender bender**. Now there's **rubber necking**.

Ian: What **rotten luck**!

Ali: We're only five blocks away. It'll be <u>quicker</u> if I let you out here and you run the rest of the way.

Ian: Okay. Here's 10 bucks. **Keep the change**.

IDIOMS & EXPRESSIONS

back roads – secondary roads; little-used roads

• Don't take the highway during rush hour. Take the **back roads** instead.

(to) break something to someone – to tell someone bad news

• I'm sorry to **break it to** you, but we're not going to get to the airport in time for your flight.

---

bumper-to-bumper traffic – heavy traffic; so much traffic that one is barely moving

• The drive into the city took us twice as long as usual due to **bumper-to-bumper traffic**.

---

close call – a near miss; something that was almost an accident

• A truck entered our lane without signaling, and we had a **close call**.

---

fender bender – a small crash between two vehicles

• Last night I had a **fender bender** in the parking garage, so today I'm taking my car to the repair shop.

NOTE: fenders are the panels above the front wheels of a car

(to) get pulled over – to get stopped by the police

• Natasha **got pulled over** for going through a stop sign.

Hop in! – Get in the car!

• You need a ride to school? **Hop in!**

(to) keep the change – to keep the difference between the charge and the money a customer is giving

• The bill at the restaurant came to $17. We gave the waitress a twenty and told her to **keep the change**.

rotten luck – bad luck

• I can't believe I've got a flat tire. I've had nothing but **rotten luck** all day today.

---

rubber necking – when cars slow down to look at an accident

• A truck was lying on its side on the highway, and traffic was backed up for miles due to **rubber necking**.

(to) step on it – to go faster (refers to stepping on the gas pedal)

• There's a creepy man following close behind us. Let's **step on it** and get away from him!

---

traffic is heavy – there are lot of cars on the road, so the driving is slow

• **Traffic was heavy** on Route 9 this morning due to an accident.

---

up ahead – in front of (someone); in the near distance

• I see an ambulance **up ahead**. There must've been an accident.

Where are you headed? – Where are you going?

• "**Where are you headed?**" — "I'm going to the mall."

✑ Practice the Expressions

Choose the best substitute for the phrase or sentence in bold:

1) I had a **fender bender** on my way home from work yesterday.
   a) major crash
   b) small crash
   c) broken fender

2) If everybody would stop **rubber necking**, traffic would start moving a lot faster.
   a) slowing down to look at an accident
   b) driving so carefully
   c) looking at what's going on all around

3) I owe you nine dollars. Here's ten. **Keep the change.**
   a) Give me back one dollar.
   b) Give me change when you have it.
   c) Keep the dollar.

4) You got a flat tire. **What rotten luck!**
   a) How unfortunate!
   b) How fortunate!
   c) How strange!

5) Ninth and Grand Street? **Hop in!**
   a) Go that way!
   b) Get in the taxi!
   c) Over there!

6) I hate to **break it to you**, but this relationship isn't working.
   a) tell you something you already know
   b) give you the good news
   c) give you the bad news

7) Pam got **pulled over** for talking on her cellphone while driving.
   a) thrown in jail
   b) in an accident
   c) stopped by the police

8) A dog ran into the road, and I **had a close call**.
   a) almost hit it
   b) ran it over
   c) told it to move

9) **Where are you headed?**
   a) Where were you?
   b) Where are you?
   c) Where are you going?

10) I see an accident **up ahead**.
   a) in front of us
   b) behind us
   c) to the side

Language Lens: Comparative & Superlatives Adjectives

Comparative Adjectives

Use a comparative adjective to compare two things or people. The word "than" comes before the object of the comparison.

Examples:
• This mug is bigger than that one.
• My laptop was more expensive than yours.
• I thought Jane was older. (Note: here the comparison is implied. I thought Jane was older *than she really is*).

Form the comparative like this:

With short words (1-2 syllables): add –er to the end of the words. If the last two letters of the word are a vowel + consonant, double the final consonant before adding –er.

Examples:

big ➜ bigger

hot ➜ hotter

If the word ends in "y," change the "y" to "i" before adding –er.

Examples:

pretty ➜ prettier

ugly ➜ uglier

With longer words (many 2 syllable words and all 3+ syllable words): add "less" or "more" before the word.

Examples:

graceful ➜ more graceful

intelligent ➜ more intelligent

qualified ➜ less qualified

interested ➜ less interested

Superlative adjectives

Use a superlative adjective to express that something or someone is the most extreme example of something. The word "the" is very often used before superlative adjectives.

Examples:
• Jennifer thinks the iPad is the best tablet computer.
• That was the most interesting movie I've ever seen!
• The biggest pumpkin ever weighed 1,502 pounds.
• That was the worst meal I ever ate.

⇒ While you use a comparative when you are comparing two people or things, you use a superlative when you have **three or more** people or things.

Examples:
• Andrea is the smartest person in her class.
• Of the four job candidates, Alex is the most qualified.

Form the superlative like this:
With short words (1-2 syllables): add –est to the end of the words. If the last two letters of the word are a vowel + consonant, double the final consonant before adding –est.
big ➔ biggest
hot ➔ hottest

When the word ends in a "y", change the "y" to "i" before adding the –est.
pretty ➔ prettiest
ugly ➔ ugliest
scary ➔ scariest

With longer words (many 2 syllable words and all 3+ syllable words): add "least" or "most" before the word.
graceful ➔ most graceful
beautiful ➔ most beautiful
qualified ➔ most qualified

Irregular comparative / superlative forms

Some comparatives and superlatives do not follow the usual pattern. Here are the most common irregular forms:

	Comparative	Superlative
good	better	best
bad	worse	worst
less	lesser	least
little (amount)	less	least
many	more	most
far (distance)	farther	farthest
far (extent)	further	furthest

Examples:

• Jason drives an hour to get to work. Of all our employees, he lives the farthest away.

• Of all the schools he applied to, Tim is least interested in attending the University of Vermont.

• You didn't get a raise this year? Things could be worse. At least you still have your job.

• Of all the jobs I applied for, I'm most excited about the one at Google.

• You think I'm interested in dating my boss? Nothing could be further from the truth!

• Adam is by far the best website designer I know.

Quick Quiz

Fill in the blanks with the missing word or words:

1) Vince is a _____ golfer than Nick.

   a) best   b) better   c) more good

2) Neptune is the _____ planet from Earth.

   a) furthest   b) farthest   c) further

3) Your salary is _____ than mine.

   a) high   b) more high   c) higher

4) That was the _____ movie I've ever seen!

   a) bad   b) worse   c) worst

5) Natalie is _____ than her sister.

   a) prettiest   b) more pretty   c) prettier

6) I don't know who's _____, Monica or Terry.

   a) more interesting   b) most interesting   c) interesting

7) Brandon bought his fiancée the _____ ring in the store.

   a) expensivest   b) most expensive   c) expensiver

8) Of all the questions on the test, the last one was the _____.

   a) more difficult   b) most difficult   c) difficultest

9) We have two good candidates for the position. Now we need to figure out who's _____.

   a) more qualified   b) most qualified   c) qualifiedest

10) Joel earns _____ money than his younger brother.

   a) less   b) lesser   c) the least

MAKING EXCUSES

Mary and her husband Jake are supposed to go to Erica's for dinner tomorrow night. But then Mary remembers that Jake told her they were going to his boss's house for a party at the same time. Mary apologizes to Erica for backing out of the dinner.

Mary: Erica, I hate to **back out at the eleventh hour**, but Jake and I aren't going to be able to **make it** to your **dinner party** tomorrow night.

Erica: **What a shame! Did something come up?**

Mary: Yes, we have to go to a party at Jake's boss's house. Jake had told me about it a couple of weeks ago, but **it slipped my mind**.

Erica: You're going to be **missing out on** a great meal. I'm making duck with olives and couscous. I already bought the duck.

Mary: You better freeze some of it! I **feel awful**. You must think I'm the biggest **flake**!

Erica: **Don't sweat it. These things happen.**

Mary: Let me **make it up to** you. I'd like you and Alex to come to dinner at our place next Saturday.

Erica: Okay, **that sounds good** ... oh, I just remembered. Alex's parents are visiting for the weekend.

Mary: Bring them along too. **The more the merrier!**

Erica: I'd better check with Alex. I'll call you later today to *confirm*.

IDIOMS & EXPRESSIONS

at the eleventh hour – at the last minute

• Ken and Dana were supposed to get married on Saturday, but he got nervous **at the eleventh hour** and canceled the wedding.

(to) back out – to break an engagement, appointment, promise, or agreement

• I know I promised to drive you to the airport on Friday, but now I'm going to have to **back out**.

NOTE: "back out" is often followed by "of": Kathy agreed to host an exchange student, but now she's trying to back out <u>of</u> it.

Did something come up? – Did something unexpected happen?

• "I'm sorry I won't be able to make it to your party on Friday." — **"Did something come up?"**

dinner party – a social event at someone's house in which dinner is served

• I'm having a **dinner party** on Saturday, and I'm calling to see if you're free.

Don't sweat it – don't worry about it

• "I'm really sorry, but I can't pick you up from the airport on Saturday." — **"Don't sweat it."**

flake – an unreliable person; someone you can't count on

• Cindy asked me to call her at 8 o'clock last night and when I called, her husband said she was out with a friend. What a **flake**!

NOTE: The adjective form is "flaky."

I feel awful – I'm sorry about the situation (often said to express that you know you've done something wrong)

• You got sick from the tuna salad I made? **I feel awful**!

146

it slipped my mind – I forgot

• I'm sorry I forgot to mail the package. **It slipped my mind**.

(to) make it – to come; to be present

• I'm not sure if I'll be able to **make it** to the staff meeting on Wednesday morning.

(to) make it up to someone – to do something nice for someone (after you've done something that was not so nice, such as canceling on someone)

• I'm sorry I forgot your birthday. Let me **make it up to** you and take you out for a drink tonight.

(to) miss out (on) – see Lesson 3

that sounds good – I like your suggestion

• "We're planning to bring a bottle of wine when we come to your house for dinner on Saturday." — "**That sounds good**."

NOTE: You can say this to answer positively when you are offered something or asked your opinion.

the more the merrier – the more people who participate in an event or activity, the more fun it'll be for everyone (often said to encourage somebody to participate)

• We already have 15 people in our book club, but you should join too. **The more the merrier**.

these things happen – sometimes things happen that you can't control

• You forgot your wallet? Don't worry about it. **These things happen**. I'll pay for lunch today.

What a shame! – that's too bad; how unfortunate

• "Scott broke his leg, so he won't be able to go on the class ski trip." — "**What a shame!**"

🖎 Practice the Expressions

Fill in the blanks using the following expressions:

slipped her mind	what a shame	make it
at the eleventh hour	these things happen	
did something come up	make it up to us	
the more the merrier	dinner party	flake

Erica: Bad news. Jake and Mary can't (1) tomorrow night.

Alex: (2) ! I was really looking forward to having them at the (3) .

Erica: I know, but what can we do? (4) .

Alex: Why can't they make it? (5) ?

Erica: Yes. It turns out they have a dinner at Jake's boss's house tomorrow night.

Alex: I can't believe they're canceling (6) . Didn't she know about the other dinner before?

Erica: Yes, Jake had told her about it, but it (7) .

Alex: What a (8) !

Erica: She was very apologetic. She wants to (9) by having us over next week.

Alex: My parents are going to be here, remember?

Erica: Mary said we should bring them too. " (10) ," she said.

Language Lens: "had better"

Use "had better" to offer **advice** or **suggestions** or to say what one **should do** in a certain situation — in other words, what the sensible or smart thing to do would be. To say what one should <u>not</u> do, use "had better not."

> **Form it like this:**
> had (or 'd) + better + base form of verb
> had (or 'd) + better not + base form of verb

The contractions (you'd better leave / I'd better leave) are much more common than the full forms (you had better leave / I had better leave).

Examples:
• You'd better finish your homework before going out tonight.
• You'd better not drive if it's snowing heavily.
• You'd better not ask your father for any more money.
• We'd better check the weather before we leave on our ski trip.
• I'd better call my wife so she knows I'll be home late.
• I'd better let you move the couch. I don't want to hurt my back.
• I'm on a diet. I'd better not have another cookie.
• It's already midnight? I'd better go to bed!

When speaking, people often leave out the word "had" (or the 'd):
Examples:
• You better turn down that music!
• You better go to sleep now.
• You better start paying attention in class.
• We better buy your plane tickets today.

Quick Quiz

Complete the sentences with the verbs indicated below. Use the contraction for had better ('d better):

Example:
You _____ a gym and start exercising! (join)

Answer: You'd better join a gym and start exercising!

1) If you've got to be at work by 9, you _____ now! (leave)

2) You _____ all night surfing the Internet again! (not stay up)

3) If you want to lose 25 pounds, you _____ eating so much junk food. (stop)

4) We _____ a light on in the house when we go on vacation. (leave)

5) You _____ that video on YouTube for the whole world to see! (not post)

6) You _____ those mushrooms you picked are edible! (make sure)

7) We _____ the gas tank before leaving on our road trip. (fill up)

8) You're worried about getting lost? You _____ me! (follow)

9) You _____ with Chris before borrowing his iPod. (check)

10) You _____ on another date with that guy! (not go)

RUNNING LATE

Anna apologizes for being late to a meeting. Rich is angry that she's late, but their colleague Kyle suggests they stop discussing it and start the meeting.

Anna: I'm sorry I'm late. I hope I didn't **hold up** the meeting.

Rich: We've all been here <u>since</u> 9 o'clock. We've been waiting here <u>for</u> half an hour!

Anna: I'm sorry to **keep you waiting**.

Rich: Anna, I'm **onto** you. You're always late!

Anna: I was meeting with a client **across town** and that meeting **ran over**.

Rich: **It's always one excuse after another with you,** Anna. We've all got busy schedules.

Kyle: Rich, don't **make a mountain out of a molehill**. Anna apologized for being late.

Rich: Next time you're **running late, give me a head's up**. I believe you have my phone number.

Anna: I didn't realize that being 20 minutes late was going to be such a **big deal**.

Kyle: I suggest we **get the ball rolling**. We're already **running behind**.

Anna: Good idea!

IDIOMS & EXPRESSIONS

across town – on the other side of town

• The restaurant you suggested is **across town**. Can you recommend someplace closer?

big deal – a problem; an issue

• When Paul's pipes leaked and his kitchen flooded, it was a **big deal**.

(to) get the ball rolling – to get started

• Emily and Tracy came up with a great idea for a new business, but they're not sure how to **get the ball rolling**.

(to) give someone a head's up – to let someone know in advance

• Let me **give you a head's up**. Ben is going to be calling you later this week for some career advice.

(to) hold up – to delay

• If I'm not at your office at 11, please don't **hold up** the meeting. I'll come as soon as I can.

It's always one excuse after another with you – you never take the blame for things, instead you give an excuse

• Last night you couldn't clean up after dinner because you had homework. Tonight, you can't clean up because you have soccer practice. **It's always one excuse after another with you**.

(to) keep someone waiting – to be late for an appointment, causing the person you are meeting with to wait

• I'm a few minutes late. Sorry to **keep you waiting**.

(to) make a mountain out of a molehill – to make a big deal out of something small; to get upset about a small issue

• I already apologized for forgetting to deposit the check. Don't **make a mountain out of a molehill**.

(to be) onto someone – to be aware of someone's behavior; to be suspicious of someone about something • I know Bill spends half his day on job search websites. I'm **onto** him.
(to) run behind – to be behind schedule • The hair stylist told me she was **running behind** because her previous client showed up 20 minutes late.
(to) run late – to be late; to start something later than scheduled • I'm calling my boss to tell her I'm **running late** and won't be in the office until 9:30.
(to) run over – to last longer than scheduled (referring to meetings, interviews, etc.) • The meeting **ran over** by 15 minutes.

✍ Practice the Expressions

Choose the most appropriate response to the following:

1) Let's get started with the presentations now instead of waiting for everybody to show up.
   a) Yes, let's hold up the meeting for everybody.
   b) Good thinking. We should plan on running late today.
   c) Good idea. It's time to get the ball rolling.

2) Do you think it'll take us 45 minutes to get to the restaurant?
   a) Yes, it's a big deal.
   b) Yes, we're running behind.
   c) Yes, it's across town.

3) This meeting was supposed to end at 3 and it's already 3:30.
   a) So we won't be running behind today.
   b) So we won't be running over.
   c) So we've already run over by half an hour.

4) Just to let you know, the company president will be dropping by our offices at 4:30 today.
   a) Okay, thanks for giving me a head's up.
   b) Okay, thanks for getting the ball rolling.
   c) Okay, maybe he'll be running behind.

5) Julia showed up two hours late this morning, and she was wearing a very nice suit.
   a) It's always one excuse after another with her.
   b) I'm onto her. She's looking for another job.
   c) Thanks for getting the ball rolling.

6) My meeting lasted an hour longer than I expected.
   a) So you must be running behind now.
   b) So you must be running over now.
   c) So you must be getting the ball rolling now.

7) I'm upset. You had lunch with our boss, and you didn't invite me?
   a) That's right. I'm onto you.
   b) It's always one excuse after another with you.
   c) Please don't make a mountain out of a molehill.

8) I'm calling to let you know I'll be a little late to our meeting.
   a) Thanks for letting me know you're running late.
   b) Thanks for getting the ball rolling.
   c) Thanks for running over by 30 minutes.

9) Yesterday I was late because my car broke down. Today I was late because my alarm clock broke.
   a) Don't make a mountain out of a molehill.
   b) It's always one excuse after another with you.
   c) I'm glad you gave me a head's up.

10) Finally! You're 25 minutes late for our meeting.
    a) Sorry to keep you waiting.
    b) Sorry you're running behind.
    c) Sorry you're running over.

Language Lens: For/Since

Since and for both introduce periods of time.

⇒ **Since refers to the time period when something began.** Use since when referring to a specific time period, time of day, or date:
- since 1995
- since 11 a.m. yesterday
- since last year
- since the Renaissance

Examples with since:
- We've been living in Chicago since 1996. (specific time = since)
- I've been in Paris since last Monday, and I'm leaving tomorrow. (specific time = since)
- Jen has been watching TV since 5 o'clock. (specific time = since)
Note: You will never use since + ago. We've been running this business since last year. (NOT: since one year ago)

⇒ **For is used to express the duration (or length) of the activity.**
- for two years
- for an hour
- for decades

Examples with for:
- We have been living in Chicago for ten years. (duration = for)
- I'll be in Paris for a week. (duration = for)
- I'll be out of the office for several hours. (duration = for)

Common expressions with since and for:
- Joan has been studying Chinese **for ages**, and she still doesn't speak it well! (for ages = for a very long time)
- We'll be staying in this apartment **for the time being**. (for the time being = for now; for a while)
- **Since when** do you wear perfume to school? (since when = When did you start doing that?)
- **Ever since** you told me that Cindy likes to gossip, I haven't told her anything. (ever since = starting when; since the time when)

Quick Quiz

Fill in the blanks with the missing word:

1) Michelle has been studying Spanish _____ five years.

    a) since   b) for

2) Roger has had the flu _____ last Wednesday and hasn't been able to go to work.

    a) since   b) for

3) Paul will be studying at Harvard _____ another semester.

    a) since   b) for

4) I haven't been to St. Petersburg _____ 2004.

    a) since   b) for

5) Greg has worked at Dell _____ ten years.

    a) since   b) for

6) Hank's Electronics has been in business _____ 1969.

    a) since   b) for

7) Juan has lived in the United States _____ five years.

    a) since   b) for

8) Bob has been in London _____ last Tuesday.

    a) since   b) for

9) I'll be out of the office _____ 10 days.

    a) since   b) for

10) _____ when did you start wearing jeans to work?

    a) Since   b) For

DOWN ON ONE'S LUCK

Steve runs into his old friend Carl and asks how he's doing. Carl tells him that he's lost his job and he's got no money. Steve offers him a short-term job at his company.

Steve: Hi, Carl. **Long time no see**. How've you been?

Carl: **Down on my luck**! I **got laid off** six months ago, and now I'm **flat broke**.

Steve: Sorry to hear that. Is your wife still working?

Carl: Yes, but she's only making **minimum wage**.

Steve: It's hard to **get by** on that!

Carl: **Tell me about it!** We're so **cash-strapped**, we're going to need to sell our house.

Steve: What type of job are you looking for?

Carl: I'm **exploring all avenues**. Marketing, sales…

Steve: <u>I wish you'd told</u> me earlier. We just hired a new marketing manager!

Carl: <u>I wish I'd known</u> about that job.

Steve: We still need some help in our sales department. It would only be **short term**, but it would help you **get back on your feet**.

Carl: I'm definitely interested.

Steve: The job does involve a lot of **grunt work**.

Carl: That's fine. **Beggars can't be choosers**.

beggars can't be choosers – you can't always get exactly what you want; when you need something badly, you're willing to take whatever you can get

• I know you don't like Al's Pizza, but it's the only place that's still open this late. **Beggars can't be choosers**.

cash-strapped – having very little money; not having enough money

• Joel has agreed to lend his **cash-strapped** son $5,000 to cover his rent for the next few months.

(to be) down on one's luck – in a period of bad luck (especially regarding finances)

• After being **down on his luck** for months, Ken finally got a new job and has started dating a lovely woman.

(to) explore all avenues – to consider many possibilities

• Kyle just graduated from college and is now **exploring all avenues**, including jobs at banks and with the government.

flat broke – without any money; poor

• Dan would like to move out of his parent's house, but he can't afford to. He's **flat broke**.

(to) get back on one's feet – to recover; to have sufficient money

• You lost your job and are having trouble paying your rent? I hope you **get back on your feet** soon!

(to) get by – to survive; to live from

• Jay's wife Susan lost her job, but the family is able to **get by** on just his salary.

(to) get laid off – to lose one's job; to get fired or let go from work

• After Scott **got laid off** from Ford, it took him six months to find a new job.

grunt work – work requiring little skill; menial work

• "Did Angela enjoy her summer internship at the bank?" — "No, she was stuck doing **grunt work** like making copies and getting coffee for the managers."

long time no see – we haven't seen each other in a long time

• Hi, Tracy. **Long time no see.** What have you been up to for the past couple of years?

minimum wage – the minimum amount an employer can pay an employee, according to U.S. law

• Right now Emily is making **minimum wage** at the fast food restaurant, but she's hoping to get a raise soon.

short term – not permanent; for a certain period of time only

• Ryan's company offered him a **short-term** assignment in Beijing. He'll be there for six months.

Tell me about it! – I agree

• "The professor's lecture sure was boring." — "**Tell me about it!** I fell asleep after 10 minutes."

✎ Practice the Expressions

Fill in the blanks with the missing word:

1) Ashley isn't sure what she wants to do when she graduates from college. She plans to explore all ____.

    a) avenues   b) streets   c) lanes

2) During his internship at the magazine, Justin got stuck doing lots of ____ work like making copies and buying supplies.

   a) slave   b) groan   c) grunt

3) Tim lost his job a few months ago at the auto plant, and now he's ____ broke.

   a) plain   b) flat   c) cash

4) After Hurricane Katrina, many families had trouble getting back on their ____.

   a) legs   b) toes   c) feet

5) During the marathon, somebody handed Jack a cup of warm water. He would've preferred cold water, but ____ can't be choosers.

   a) runners   b) beggars   c) vagrants

6) "This food is too spicy!" — "____ me about it. My mouth is on fire!"

   a) Say   b) Tell   c) Talk to

7) When Emily told her father she was ____-strapped, he offered to lend her some money.

   a) dollar   b) financial   c) cash

8) It's hard to live in San Francisco and get ____ on a teacher's salary.

   a) around   b) through   c) by

9) Greg got laid ____, and he's now looking for a new job.

   a) off   b) on   c) through

10) Angela is only working as a waitress short ____. Next month, she's starting a new job in sales.

   a) time   b) term   c) period

Language Lens: Wish statements

Use "wish" to say that you want a situation to be different than it is. You can use "wish" for situations in the present and in the past.

⇒ **Present: To talk about the present, use:**
wish + verb in the past tense

Examples:
• I wish I had a summer house (I don't have one).
• I wish I spoke Chinese (I don't speak Chinese).
• I wish I were* rich (I'm not rich).
• I wish you were* a lawyer (You're not a lawyer).

* After "wish" use "were" instead of "was". This is the form of the verb "to be" that's used when situations are imagined or unreal. It's called the subjunctive.

To say that you are not happy with the current situation and that you want somebody else to do something about it, use:
wish + would (or the contraction 'd) + base form of the verb

Examples:
• I wish you would lose a few pounds.
• I wish that guy I met at the bar would call me!
• I wish they'd stop talking during the movie.
• I wish it would stop snowing.*

*In this case, you need Mother Nature to help you change the situation!

⇒ **Past: To talk about situations in the past that you regret or are not happy about, use:**
wish + had (or 'd) / hadn't + verb in the past tense

Examples:
• I wish I hadn't agreed to this.
• I wish I'd followed your directions.
• I wish I hadn't eaten that sushi.
• She wishes she'd gotten into the University of Pennsylvania.

Quick Quiz

Fill in the blanks with the missing word or words:

1) I can't sleep. I wish I _____ that scary movie before going to bed.
   a) hadn't watched   b) couldn't watch   c) don't watch

2) Greg is flat broke. I wish I _____ some money to lend him.
   a) have   b) had   c) am having

3) I love to swim. I wish I _____ a fish.
   a) would be   b) will be   c) were

4) I wish I _____ more than minimum wage.
   a) earn   b) earned   c) am earning

5) Jim wishes he _____ a date for the school dance.
   a) has   b) had   c) would have

6) I wish you _____ your friends not to call so late.
   a) told   b) tell   c) would tell

7) Your hair looks messy. I wish you _____ a haircut.
   a) would get   b) got   c) get

8) Spanish is so useful. I wish I _____ Spanish!
   a) speak   b) spoke   c) would speak

9) I wish my husband _____ riding a motorcycle. It's so dangerous!
   a) stopped   b) would stop   c) had stopped

10) Rick is not doing well in school. I wish he _____ more.
   a) would study   b) studies   c) will study

REACTING TO BAD NEWS

Jenny runs into her friend Carol in the supermarket. Jenny asks Carol how she's been and Carol tells her all her bad news. Jenny responds with sympathy and offers her support.

Jenny: Hi, Carol. **How's life been treating you?**

Carol: **I've been better**. I'm **going through a rough patch**.

Jenny: **Sorry to hear that**. What's going on?

Carol: My husband and I are **splitting up**. I **found out** he's been **cheating on** me for years with his receptionist.

Jenny: I'm **speechless**!

Carol: Fortunately, I wasn't **speechless** when I found out. I **gave him a piece of my mind**!

Jenny: Good! And how's your son John doing? Did he <u>manage to find</u> a job since we last spoke?

Carol: **No such luck**. Poor John fell off the roof a couple weeks ago while doing some repairs and broke both his legs!

Jenny: You must've been **beside yourself**!

Carol: I was a **basket case** for several days. Now he's **on the road to recovery**, but it's going to take a while.

Jenny: If you ever <u>want to talk,</u> just give me a call.

Carol: I would <u>enjoy **getting**</u> together.

Jenny: Okay. I'll **stop by** later this week.

IDIOMS & EXPRESSIONS

basket case – an emotional and/or physical mess

• After her house burned down, Donna was a **basket case**.

beside oneself – very upset

• When Tracy's boss told her she wasn't doing a good job, she was **beside herself**.

(to) cheat on someone – to have romantic relations on the side, with somebody other than one's partner

• After Nancy read the text messages on her husband's cell phone, she realized he was **cheating on** her.

(to) find out – to discover facts about someone or something

• I just **found out** that Tanya is pregnant.

(to) get together – to meet with someone (usually socially)

• I'd love to **get together** on Saturday if you have time.

(to) give someone a piece of one's mind – see Lesson 16

(to) go through a rough patch – to have a lot of problems during a time period; to experience a period of bad luck

• Joe lost his job last week and this week his girlfriend broke up with him. He's **going through a rough patch**.

How's life been treating you? – How are you?; How've you been?

• "**How's life been treating you?**" — "Can't complain."

I've been better – things are not going well for me

• "How are you doing?" — "**I've been better**."

no such luck – we haven't had good fortune in that area; we haven't been so lucky

• "Did your boss let you out early for the holiday weekend?" — "**No such luck**."

on the road to recovery – starting to get better • Stephanie was sick with the flu for a week, but now she's **on the road to recovery**.
(I'm) sorry to hear that – that's too bad; I feel bad for you • "I got fired yesterday." — "**Sorry to hear that**."
speechless – unable to speak due to surprise; shocked • After being fined $300 for a speeding ticket, Wendy was **speechless**.
(to) split up – to break up; to end a marriage or other intimate relationship • After years of fighting, Irene and her husband finally **split up**.
(to) stop by – come over (often for a short visit) • If you're in my neighborhood on Saturday, please **stop by**.

✍ Practice the Expressions

Choose the most appropriate response to the following:

1) Did you know that Sara and her husband are splitting up?
   a) No, what are they splitting?
   b) No, do you know what happened?
   c) No, why didn't anybody tell me this good news?

2) If you get a chance, stop by over the weekend.
   a) Okay, I'll come over.
   b) Sure, I'll stop it.
   c) Okay, I'll spend all weekend with you.

3) Nick was sick for months, but now he's on the road to recovery.
   a) I'm sorry to hear he's not improving.
   b) I'm glad to hear he's able to travel again.
   c) I'm glad to hear he's getting better.

4) Your son has dropped out of Harvard and joined the military? I'm speechless!
   a) We were very surprised too.
   b) We weren't surprised either.
   c) We agree that it's very exciting.

5) Ron just lost his job after 25 years at the same company. He's beside himself.
   a) I can understand why he's upset.
   b) Right. He was ready to leave that job.
   c) I'm glad to hear he isn't too upset.

6) Brenda just found out that her husband has been cheating on her for years with his secretary.
   a) Do you think she'll leave him?
   b) Do you think Brenda likes the secretary?
   c) Do you think she's happy about this?

7) Grace has been a basket case since losing her job.
   a) I'm glad she's doing well.
   b) I hope she'll start feeling better soon.
   c) She didn't really like that job anyway.

8) I was hoping I'd win the big lottery jackpot, but no such luck.
   a) You won? Congratulations!
   b) You didn't win? That's surprising.
   c) Oh well. There's always next time!

9) You've been sick all week? Sorry to hear that.
   a) Thanks.
   b) Sorry I told you.
   c) You could be more sympathetic.

10) I've been going through a rough patch lately.
    a) Things have been fine with me too.
    b) I'm glad to hear it.
    c) Sorry to hear that. What's going on?

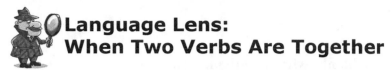

Language Lens:
When Two Verbs Are Together

When there are two verbs in a row (one after the other), the second verb is sometimes in the infinitive form ("to" form) and sometimes in the gerund form (ending in –ing). The first verb determines (Verb 1) the form of the second verb (Verb 2). Study these two tables with common verbs.

Verb 1 + Verb 2 in the Infinitive ("to" form)	
Verb 1	Verb 2 is in the infinitive
agree	I agreed **to pick** Sue up from the airport.
cause	What caused Nick **to break** out in a rash?
deserve	We deserve **to know** why the company is closing.
expect	When does your son expect **to graduate**?
hope	We hope **to visit** some castles on our trip to Ireland.
learn	Lisa learned **to ski** on her vacation.
offer	Please offer **to help** bake cookies for the bake sale.
manage	Did you manage **to get** to the airport on time?
promise	I promise **to call** you as soon as we arrive in Paris.
want	What do you want **to do** this weekend?

Verb 1 + Verb 2 in the Gerund (-ing form)	
Verb 1	Verb 2 is a gerund
appreciate	We appreciated **having** a great tour guide in China.
avoid	Let's avoid **getting** food poisoning on our trip.
consider	We considered **renting** instead of buying a house.
enjoy	John enjoys **surfing** in Big Sur.
feel like	What do you feel like **doing** today?
finish	When you finish **watching** the movie, let me know.
mind	Do you mind **going** to the store?
recommend	I recommend **exploring** Chicago by foot.
suggest	I suggest **building** a new website.
think	You think **getting** a medical degree is easy?

Quick Quiz

Fill in the blanks with the missing word:

1) I suggest _____ Bratislava while you're on your tour of Europe.
   a) to visit   b) visiting

2) If you're on a diet, I recommend _____ canola oil instead of butter when baking.
   a) to use   b) using

3) Did you manage _____ a plumber to fix your sink on Saturday?
   a) finding   b) to find

4) On the weekends, Ed enjoys _____ novels and watching videos.
   a) reading   b) to read

5) I promised Erica I'd get a drink with her after work, and now I don't feel like _____.
   a) to go   b) going

6) Do you promise _____ me when I'm working abroad in London?
   a) visiting   b) to visit

7) When do you expect _____ the repair work on my car?
   a) to finish   b) finishing

8) We want _____ to New York next year.
   a) moving   b) to move

9) Do you mind _____ Jesse from the airport on Saturday?
   a) to pick up   b) picking up

10) I think _____ a night in Santa Barbara on our way to Los Angeles is a good idea.
   a) spending   b) to spend

Glossary

baggy – not fitting closely; too loose

compact – a small car (smaller than a mid-size car)

confirm – to let one know for sure; to make firm

convention – a large meeting, bringing together people who share a common personal or professional interest

discolored – changed from its natural color (often darker)

expire – come to an end (subscriptions, membership plans)

filling – material which covers the cavity of a tooth

frustrating – annoying; discouraging

molar – the big teeth in the back of the mouth

reception – the strength of a signal (regarding cell phones, TV, etc)

reimburse – to pay someone back for an expense

replacement – something or someone that takes the place of another

sensitive – easily irritated

server – waiter; waitress

snug – close-fitting; tight

unloaded – taken out from storage (such as from a trunk or airplane)

Answer Key

LESSON 1:

Practice the Expressions

1. b   2. a   3. c   4. c   5. a   6. a   7. c   8. b   9. b   10. a

Quiz Quiz

1. isn't it
2. isn't he
3. aren't you
4. don't they
5. weren't you
6. is it
7. can you
8. shouldn't you
9. can't you
10. should we

LESSON 2:

Practice the Expressions

1. steer clear of
2. What a bummer
3. take a crack at it
4. to the letter
5. let alone
6. has the magic touch
7. issue you a credit
8. works out
9. even exchange
10. don't hesitate to

Quiz Quiz

1. a   2. a   3. b   4. a   5. b   6. b   7. a   8. b   9. b   10. a

LESSON 3:

Practice the Expressions

1. lemon
2. in mint condition
3. miss out
4. swing by
5. taking it for a test drive
6. reach an agreement
7. split the difference
8. haggle
9. steal
10. You've got a deal

Quiz Quiz

1. a   2. c   3. b   4. c   5. a   6. a   7. b   8. b   9. a   10. c

LESSON 4:

Practice the Expressions

1. a   2. c   3. b   4. b   5. c   6. b   7. c   8. a   9. b   10. b

Quiz Quiz

Part A:

1. Yes, I do.
2. No, I don't.
3. No, she didn't.
4. Yes, they are.
5. No, he isn't.

Part B:

1. Aren't you moving to San Francisco?
2. Aren't they going to New York today?
3. Aren't you thirsty?
4. Don't you want another piece of pizza?
5. Didn't she break her arm?

LESSON 5:

Practice the Expressions

1. c   2. a   3. b   4. c   5. c   6. a   7. c   8. b   9. b   10. a

Quiz Quiz

1. Let's eat lunch at the mall.
2. Why don't we look for a birthday present for Marina?
3. How about getting some burritos for dinner?
4. Let's visit the Picasso exhibit at the Metropolitan Museum.
5. Why don't we go to Martha's Vineyard in July?
6. Let's get a subscription to *New York* magazine.
7. How about showing me how to use Skype?
8. Why don't we see a performance at Carnegie Hall?
9. Why don't we order Korean food for dinner?
10. Let's go to Italy this summer.

LESSON 6:

Practice the Expressions

1. b   2. b   3. b   4. a   5. c   6. a   7. c   8. b   9. b   10. c

Quiz Quiz

1. I was wondering if you could feed our dogs while we're away.
2. I was wondering if you could pick me up from the airport on Friday.
3. I was wondering if I could borrow your car.
4. I was wondering if you could return my library book.
5. Would you mind loaning me your laptop?
6. Would you mind turning down the music?
7. Would you mind picking up my clothes from the dry cleaners?

171

8. Could you show me how to design a website?

9. Could you please let Jim know we're running late?

10. Could you call the theater and reserve tickets?

LESSON 7:

Practice the Expressions

1. so-so	6. on me
2. went downhill	7. pick up the tab
3. put out	8. leaves a lot to be desired
4. Let's go Dutch	9. it's my treat
5. cheapskate	10. When hell freezes over

Quiz Quiz

1. How am I supposed to do my homework when it's so noisy in the house?

2. Weren't you supposed to tell me when it was time to get off the highway?

3. Who's supposed to do all the cooking for the big party you're planning?

4. Who's supposed to clean up this mess?

5. We were supposed to go to London last month, but the trip got canceled.

6. Venice is supposed to be the most beautiful city in Europe.

7. If you want to take vacation time, you're supposed to get permission from your boss.

8. Amanda and I were supposed to meet yesterday, but she canceled the meeting.

9. Who's supposed to clean all these dishes in the sink?

10. You're not supposed to take flash pictures inside the museum.

LESSON 8:

Practice the Expressions

1. What can I get for you

2. meal deal

3. pass on

4. side order

5. go light on it

6. for here or to go

7. On second thought

8. No worries

9. at no extra charge

10. Your total comes to

Quiz Quiz
Part A:
1. I'd like that report on my desk by 5 o'clock.
2. I'd like a cup of coffee.
3. I'd like to leave early on Friday.
4. I'd like another pillow.
5. I'd like some help with this project.

Part B:
1. Would you like another cup of coffee? OR: Would you like some more coffee?
2. Would you like a ride to work tomorrow? OR: Would you like me to give you a ride to work tomorrow?
3. Would you like me to look after your kids tonight? OR: Would you like me to babysit tonight?
4. Would you like me to get you a cappuccino? OR: Would you like me to bring you back a cappuccino?
5. Would you like to come here for Thanksgiving? OR: Would you like to come to my (or our) house for Thanksgiving?

LESSON 9:

Practice the Expressions
1. b   2. b   3. c   4. a   5. c   6. a   7. b   8. c   9. b   10. a

Quiz Quiz
1. b   2. a   3. a   4. b   5. c   6. b   7. a   8. c   9. c   10. c

LESSON 10:

Practice the Expressions
1. a   2. c   3. a   4. b   5. b   6. b   7. a   8. a   9. b   10. c

Quiz Quiz
Part A:
1. We are (We're) going to rent a cottage on the beach this August.
2. What sights are you going to show your visitors?
3. We are (We're) going to move to San Francisco in July.
4. I am (I'm) going to call my doctor for an appointment.
5. Someone is going to fall on this slippery sidewalk.

Part B:
1. b   2. a   3. b   4. b   5. a

LESSON 11:

Practice the Expressions

1. c 2. a 3. c 4. a 5. b 6. c 7. b 8. c 9. c 10. a

Quick Quiz

1. What if Joe doesn't get into college?
2. What if there isn't enough snow for skiing?
3. What if the restaurant is all booked?
4. What if you don't like the movie?
5. What if our company has layoffs next year?
6. What if the store goes out of business?
7. What if we run out of candy on Halloween?
8. What if our flight is delayed?
9. What if my husband loses his job?
10. What if our house doesn't sell?

LESSON 12:

Practice the Expressions

1. c 2. b 3. c 4. a 5. b 6. b 7. a 8. c 9. a 10. c

Quiz Quiz

1. a 2. a 3. b 4. b 5. a 6. b 7. a 8. b 9. a 10. a

LESSON 13:

Practice the Expressions

1. a 2. b 3. b 4. a 5. b 6. c 7. a 8. c 9. b 10. c

Quiz Quiz
Part A:

1. You'd be better off applying to law school.
2. You'd be better off studying abroad in Beijing.
3. You'd be better off going in October. OR: You'd be better off going to India in October.
4. You'd be better off renting an apartment. OR: You'd be better off renting.
5. You'd be better off waiting. OR: You'd be better off waiting to ask her to marry you.

Part B:

1. You would've been better off buying a Mac.
2. We would've been better off opening an office in India (instead).
3. We would've been better off going to France (instead).
4. He would've been better off going to Harvard.
5. She would've been better off staying in school.

LESSON 14:

Practice the Expressions

1. look familiar
2. rings a bell
3. I can't quite place you
4. It's a small world
5. paths have crossed

6. What have you been up to
7. have a lot in common
8. It's a long story
9. grab some drinks
10. fill you in

Quiz Quiz

1. used to work
2. used to get up
3. used to arrive
4. used to wonder
5. used to dream

6. used to cook
7. used to eat
8. use to want
9. use to be
10. used to complain

LESSON 15:

Practice the Expressions

1. c   2. a   3. c   4. c   5. b   6. a   7. b   8. c   9. a   10. b

Quiz Quiz

1. b   2. b   3. b   4. c   5. b   6. c   7. c   8. b   9. c   10. a

LESSON 16:

Practice the Expressions

1. b   2. c   3. b   4. a   5. a   6. c   7. c   8. b   9. c   10. a

Quiz Quiz

1. b   2. b   3. a   4. b   5. b   6. a   7. a   8. b   9. b   10. a

LESSON 17:

Practice the Expressions

1. b   2. c   3. c   4. b   5. c   6. c   7. c   8. b   9. a   10. c

Quiz Quiz

1. b   2. a   3. b   4. a   5. b   6. b   7. b   8. b   9. a   10. b

LESSON 18:

Practice the Expressions

1. a   2. c   3. c   4. b   5. a   6. c   7. a   8. b   9. b   10. a

Quiz Quiz

1. b   2. a   3. a   4. b   5. a   6. b   7. a   8. b   9. a   10. b

LESSON 19:

Practice the Expressions

1. rewards program
2. worth my while
3. earn points
4. special offers
5. As a rule
6. check in
7. zoo
8. Just our luck
9. made a racket
10. reeked of

Quiz Quiz

1. must've run
2. must've turned
3. must've stayed
4. must've pulled
5. must've forgotten
6. must've stolen
7. must've left
8. must've driven
9. must've overslept
10. must've studied

LESSON 20:

Practice the Expressions

1. taken a wrong turn
2. like the back of your hand
3. grab a bite
4. doze off
5. made a pit stop
6. turn off
7. making good time
8. backseat driver
9. I can't help myself
10. bite my tongue

Quiz Quiz

1. I hope so.
2. I think so.
3. I'm afraid so.
4. I guess so.
5. I think so.
6. I'm afraid so.
7. I hope so.
8. I guess so.
9. I think so.
10. I hope so.

176

LESSON 21:

Practice the Expressions
1. b   2. a   3. c   4. a   5. b   6. c   7. c   8. a   9. c   10. a

Quiz Quiz
1. b   2. b   3. c   4. c   5. c   6. a   7. b   8. b   9. a   10. a

LESSON 22:

Practice the Expressions
1. make it	6. at the eleventh hour
2. What a shame	7. slipped her mind
3. dinner party	8. flake
4. These things happen	9. make it up to us
5. Did something come up	10. The more the merrier

Quiz Quiz
1. 'd better leave	6. 'd better make sure
2. 'd better not stay up	7. 'd better fill up
3. 'd better stop	8. 'd better follow
4. 'd better leave	9. 'd better check
5. 'd better not post	10. 'd better not go

LESSON 23:

Practice the Expressions
1. c   2. c   3. c   4. a   5. b   6. a   7. c   8. a   9. b   10. a

Quiz Quiz
1. b   2. a   3. b   4. a   5. b   6. a   7. b   8. a   9. b   10. a

LESSON 24:

Practice the Expressions
1. a   2. c   3. b   4. c   5. b   6. b   7. c   8. c   9. a   10. b

Quiz Quiz
1. a   2. b   3. c   4. b   5. b   6. c   7. a   8. b   9. b   10. a

LESSON 25:

Practice the Expressions
1. b   2. a   3. c   4. a   5. a   6. a   7. b   8. c   9. a   10. c

Quiz Quiz
1. b   2. b   3. b   4. a   5. b   6. b   7. a   8. b   9. b   10. a

Index

Lose Your Accent in 28 Days™ is the powerful, proven

pronunciation system that will help you lose your foreign accent in weeks — not months or years. Practice 30 minutes a day for 4 weeks and greatly improve your pronunciation. No more being asked to repeat yourself!

Discover the accent reduction system preferred by faculty and students at America's most prestigious universities, including Cornell and UC Berkeley.

Lose Your Accent in 28 Days™ features **an interactive CD-ROM** that shows you exactly how to pronounce EVERY vowel and consonant through hundreds of video clips. Research shows that a combination of audio and video is more effective for learning pronunciation than audio alone.

The **Audio CD** includes over 70 minutes of material on rhythm, stress, and everyday speech patterns. The **Workbook** offers 80 techniques for better pronunciation. You'll learn from 956 guided examples.

> *I have to let you know that I am extremely happy with the method.*
>
> – Alfredo A., Canada
>
> *I highly recommend it for anyone interested in improving their accent in American English.*
>
> – Kathryn Laurent, Language Program Manager, IOR Global Services

ORDER ONLINE: www.languagesuccesspress.com

Speak Business English Like an American will help you speak better business English — quickly and confidently. You'll learn the idioms and expressions that you hear at work. What do your colleagues, your customers or clients mean when they use expressions like **pretty penny**, **rally the troops, bite the bullet**, and **fast followers**? By studying this book and audio CD system, you'll find out...and soon you'll be using these expressions too!

> *This book is wonderful and helped me a lot. I recommend it to everyone who wants to learn more about expressions.*
> – A. Perinei, Brazil

Jump-start your career with **Speak Better Business English and Make More Money**. Americans don't speak the kind of English you'll find in textbooks or hear in most classrooms. They speak business lingo, a collection of expressions and idioms that cover marketing, finance, accounting, HR issues, strategy, and other business topics. Now you can equip yourself with this powerful lingo too!

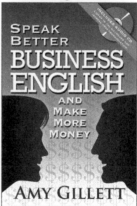

Presenting over 30 business scenarios based on real-life situations. You learn the Business English that's really spoken in today's working world. Conversations include: asking for a promotion, discussing legal issues, managing conflict, growing your business and many more. Listen to native speakers on the audio CD and improve your pronunciation.

Study together with *Speak Business English Like an American* and learn over 775 business expressions!

ORDER ONLINE: www.languagesuccesspress.com

Say it Better in English:
Useful Phrases for Work & Everyday Life
by Marianna Pascal

Say it Better in English was developed for busy people who want to improve their conversational English — fast. Learn the most common useful American English expressions for work and everyday life!

This popular ESL book teaches over 300 useful expressions. Cartoons show you how to use each expression in real-life situations. That's what makes them so easy to learn! The cartoon method has helped thousands of busy people. It can help you too. Crossword puzzles let you check your new knowledge. What a fun way to improve your conversational English!

DISCOVER OUR IPHONE & IPAD APPS!

Speak English Like an American: This bestselling app teaches over 300 American English idioms and expressions you're most likely to hear in daily life. Also available for Android.

Speak Business English 1: Based on the book *Speak Business English Like an American*, this app teaches 200 expressions you're most likely to hear at work. Listen to the audio, click on an idiom to see the definition, record yourself and play it back, and take interactive quizzes.

Speak Business English 11: Learn another set of 200 Business English expressions, with the same great functionality as the Speak Business English 1 app.

Business English Power Verbs: Master 101 of the most important Business English verbs. Get ready to power your Business English with this awesome tool!

For more information on our full line of apps, visit:
www.languagesuccessapps.com